Mathematics

Formulae and Notes
for Class 11 CBSE
Full Syllabus 2025-26

By Pavitra Gupta
B.E.

All rights reserved with author. No part of this publication may be reproduced or distributed in any form or by any means.

All the information in this book has been obtained from the sources believed to be reliable and true. Author has made his best effort in preparing the book. However, author doesn't take any responsibility if anyone suffers the damages and loss due to any reason on using this book.

Preface

It gives me great pleasure in presenting this book. It covers all the chapters of complete syllabus prescribed by CBSE for class 11 Mathematics. Some topics, which are marked by an asterisk (*) in this book, are not in the CBSE syllabus for session 2025-26 (released in April 2025). However, these topics have been covered for state boards or other exams.

This is the paperback printed version of my digital book 'Mathematics Formulae and Notes: Class 11 CBSE'. The digital book has been appreciated for complete list of formulae in them and for the ways they are presented for every concept. So, on the demand by students and teachers, I present this paperback version of the same book. The books are very helpful in the preparation of CBSE exams and other competitive exams.

It's my endeavour to keep the content as simple as possible to make it easy to understand and remember.

For the students to remember the formulae easily, the book is written just like a student makes notes in the class. It makes the book very helpful to learn and remember all concepts even though it does not contain questions for practice. Also, it becomes very useful while revising for exams.

I hope the students will be able to learn each and every formula comfortably through this book.

Pavitra Gupta

Table of Contents

Preface iii

Chapter-1   Sets 1

    1   Methods to represent a Set....................................1

    2   Types of Sets 2

        2.1   Empty Set 2

        2.2   Singleton Set..2

        2.3   Finite Set 2

        2.4   Infinite Set 2

    3   Subset 3

    4   *Power Set..3

    5   Equal and Unequal sets.......................................3

    6   Proper Subset and Superset 4

    7   Equivalent Sets 4

    8   Intervals: Subsets of set R of Real Numbers 4

    9   Universal Set 5

    10   Venn Diagram 5

    11   Operations on Sets...5

        11.1 Union of sets..5

        11.2 Intersection of sets...6

        11.3 Difference of sets...7

        11.4 Complement of set..7

    12   *Formulae for 2 sets 8

    13   *Formulae for 3 sets 8

    14   Important Concepts 9

Chapter-2   Relations and Functions 10

    1   Ordered pair...10

    2   Ordered triplet 10

    3   Cartesian Product..10

*Asterisk (*) marked article (if any) is **not** in CBSE 2025-26 syllabus.*

	4	Relation	11
	4.1	Domain	11
	4.2	Range	11
	4.3	Codomain	11
	4.4	Arrow Diagram	11
	5	Function	12
	5.1	Real Valued Function	12
	5.2	Real Function	12
	6	Some Important Functions	13
	6.1	Identity Function	13
	6.2	Constant Function	13
	6.3	Polynomial Functions	13
	6.4	Rational Function	14
	6.5	Modulus Function	14
	6.6	Signum Function	15
	6.7	Greatest Integer Function	15
	7	Algebra of Real Functions	16
	7.1	Addition	16
	7.2	Subtraction	16
	7.3	Multiplication	16
	7.4	Division	16

Chapter-3 Trigonometry 17

1 (i) $1° = \pi 180\, rad$ (ii) $1\, rad = 180\pi$ degree 17

2 Arc Length 17

3 Basic Formulae 17

4 Sum and Difference of Angles 17

5 Double Angle Formulae 18

6 Triple Angle Formulae 18

7 Half Angle Formulae 18

8 Ratio Sum or Difference Formulae 19

---

*Asterisk (*) marked article (if any) is **not** in CBSE 2025-26 syllabus.*

	9	Product Formulae	19
	10	More formulae	19
	11	Domain and Range	20
	12	*General Solutions of Trigonometric Equations	21
	13	*Law of Sines (sine rule)	21
	14	*Law of Cosines (cosine rule)	21
Chapter-4		*Principle Of Mathematical Induction	22
	1	*The Principle of Mathematical Induction	22
	2	*Steps in using Principle of Mathematical Induction	22
Chapter-5		Complex Numbers	24
	1	The imaginary number, i	24
	2	Important concept	24
	3	Complex number, $a + i\,b$	24
	4	Equality of Complex Numbers	24
	5	Comparison of Complex Numbers	24
	6	Addition of Complex Numbers	25
		6.1 Properties of Addition	25
	7	Difference of Complex Numbers	25
	8	Multiplication of Complex Numbers	25
		8.1 Properties of Multiplication	26
	9	Conjugate of Complex Number, z	26
	10	Modulus of Complex Number, $|z|$	26
	11	Other Results and formulae	26
	12	Argand Plane and Polar Form	27
	13	*Converting a complex number into Polar Form	28
Chapter-6		Linear Inequalities	29
	1	Inequality and its kinds	29
	2	Rules for solving an inequality	29
	3	Representing solution of an inequality in one variable	29

4   *Graphical solution of a Linear Inequality in two variables.. 30

5   *Graphical solution of System of Linear Inequalities in two variables................................ 31

Chapter-7   **Permutations And Combinations**.................................. 32

    1   Factorial.. 32

    2   Fundamental Principle of Counting.......................... 32

    3   Permutations (Arrangements).................................. 33

    4   Combinations (Selections)....................................... 34

Chapter-8   **Binomial Theorem**.. 35

    1   Binomial Theorem.. 35

    2   General Term... 35

    3   Middle Term.. 35

    4   r^{th} term from the end.. 35

    5   Other Results from Binomial Theorem..................... 36

Chapter-9   **Sequences and Series**.. 37

    1   Sequence... 37

    2   Series.. 37

    3   Progression.. 37

    4   Arithmetic Progression (A.P.).................................. 37

        4.1   Standard form of A.P.................................... 37

        4.2   General Term.. 38

        4.3   Sum of first n terms (S_n)........................... 38

        4.4   Some Properties of A.P. 38

    5   Arithmetic Means (AMs).. 39

    6   AM between a and b... 39

    7   Geometric Progression (G.P.).................................. 39

        7.1   Standard form of G.P.................................... 39

        7.2   General Term.. 40

        7.3   Sum of first n terms (S_n)........................... 40

        7.4   Sum to infinity of G.P. 40

*Asterisk (*) marked article (if any) is **not** in CBSE 2025-26 syllabus.*

| | | 7.5 | Some Properties of G.P. | 40 |

        7.5   Some Properties of G.P. 40

    8   Geometric Means (GMs)..............................40

    9   GM between a and b......................................41

    10   Relationship Between A.M. and G.M. 41

    11   *Sum of first n terms of special series....................41

Chapter-10   Straight Lines..42

    1   Distance between two points 42

    2   Section Formula..42

        2.1   Internal Division...................................42

        2.2   External Division..................................42

    3   Mid - Point Formula 42

    4   Centroid of Triangle 43

    5   *Incenter of Triangle 43

    6   Area of Triangle 43

    7   Slope of a Line *(m)* 43

    8   Slope of x–*axis* 43

    9   Slope of y – *axis* 44

    10   Conditions for collinearity............................44

    11   Condition for parallel and perpendicular lines 44

    12   Acute Angle (θ) between two lines 44

    13   Equations of straight lines 44

        13.1   Equations of lines parallel to x and y axes ...44

        13.2   Slope – Point Form...............................45

        13.3   Two Point Form..................................45

        13.4   Intercept Form...................................45

        13.5   Slope – intercept Form 45

        13.6   *Normal Form 45

        13.7   *Symmetric Form.................................46

    14   General Form..46

    15   Distance of a Point from a Line.......................46

---

*Asterisk (*) marked article (if any) is **not** in CBSE 2025-26 syllabus.*

	16	Distance between Two Parallel Line 46
Chapter-11		Conic Sections 47
	1	Circle 47
		1.1 Standard Equation 47
		1.2 General Equation 47
		1.3 Point lying inside, outside or on the circle .. 47
	2	Parabola 48
		2.1 Standard Equations................................ 48
	3	Ellipse 50
		3.1 Standard Equations................................ 51
	4	Hyperbola 53
		4.1 Standard Equations................................ 54
Chapter-12		Three-Dimensional Geometry 56
	1	Basic Concepts 56
	2	Distance between two points 58
	3	*Section Formula.. 58
		3.1 *Internal Division................................. 58
		3.2 *External Division................................. 58
	4	*Mid - Point Formula 59
	5	*Centroid of Triangle 59
	6	*Incenter of Triangle 59
Chapter-13		Limits.. 60
	1	Concept of Limit and its Explanation.................... 60
	2	Algebra of Limits.. 60
	3	Limit of Polynomial Function 61
		3.1 Procedure to find limit of polynomial function 61
	4	Limit of Rational Function 61
		4.1 Procedure to find limit of rational function. 62
	5	Sandwich Theorem 62
	6	Important Limits... 63

*Asterisk (*) marked article (if any) is **not** in CBSE 2025-26 syllabus.*

Chapter-14		Derivatives	64
	1	Concept of Derivatives and its Explanation	64
	2	Derivatives of some important functions	66
		2.1 Formulae	66
	3	Algebra of Derivatives	66
		3.1 Sum or Difference Rule	67
		3.2 Product Rule	67
		3.3 Quotient Rule	67
Chapter-15		*Mathematical Reasoning	68
	1	*Mathematical Statement	68
	2	*Negation of a statement	68
	3	*Compound statements	68
		3.1 *Compound statements with "And"	68
		3.2 *Compound statements with "Or"	69
		3.3 *Quantifiers and Connectives	69
		3.4 *Compound statements with "if – then"	69
		3.5 *Compound statements with "if and only if"	70
	4	*Validation of statements	70
		4.1 *Validating statement 'p and q'	70
		4.2 *Validating statement 'p or q'	70
		4.3 *Validating statement 'if p then q'	70
		4.4 *Validating statement 'p if and only if q'	71
Chapter-16		Statistics	72
	1	Measures of Central Tendency	72
	2	Measures of Dispersion	72
	3	Range	72
	4	Mean Deviation	72
		4.1 Mean Deviation from Mean	73
		4.2 Mean Deviation from Median	80
	5	Standard Deviation and Variance	83

*Asterisk (*) marked article (if any) is **not** in CBSE 2025-26 syllabus.*

	5.1	Ungrouped Data	83
	5.2	Discrete Frequency Distribution	84
	5.3	Continuous Frequency Distribution	88
	6	*Coefficient of Variation	93
Chapter-17		Probability	94
	1	Random Experiment	94
	2	Sample Space and Sample Points	94
	3	Sample space for tossing a coin	94
	4	Sample space for throwing a dice	94
	5	Event	95
	6	Types of Events	96
	7	Algebra of Events	96
	8	Exhaustive Events	97
	9	Mutually Exclusive Events	97
	10	Mutually Exclusive and Exhaustive Events	98
	11	Axiomatic Definition of Probability	98
	11.1	Axioms of Probability	98
	11.2	Conditions to assign Probabilities	99
	11.3	Other condition that follows from Axioms	99
	11.4	Probabilities for equally likely outcomes	99
	12	Results from Axiomatic approach of probability	100
Chapter-18		Supplement	101
	1	POLYNOMIALS	101
	2	MENSURATION	101
	2.1	RECTANGLE :	101
	2.2	SQUARE :	101
	2.3	PARALLELOGRAM :	101
	2.4	RHOMBUS :	102
	2.5	TRAPEZIUM :	102
	2.6	TRIANGLE :	102

*Asterisk (*) marked article (if any) is **not** in CBSE 2025-26 syllabus.*

2.7 EQUILATERAL TRIANGLE : 102

2.8 CIRCLE :..102

2.9 SECTOR of a CIRCLE : 102

2.10 SEGMENT of a CIRCLE :........................103

2.11 CUBOID: 103

2.12 CUBE:..103

2.13 CYLINDER:...103

2.14 CONE:...103

2.15 SPHERE:..104

2.16 Hemi SPHERE: 104

2.17 FRUSTUM:...104

Chapter-1   Sets

A well-defined collection of objects is known as a set.

1 Methods to represent a Set

Two methods to represent a set are:
(i) Roster or Tabular form.
(ii) Set-builder form or Rule method.

- In Roster form all the elements or members are listed and separated by commas and are enclosed within curly braces { }.
- In Set-builder form the common property of all the elements is stated. It is also enclosed within curly braces { }.

- While writing a set in roster form, only the distinct elements of the set are listed, generally. It means, no element is repeated in it.
- A set is usually denoted by an English alphabet in capitals like, A, B, C, X, Y, Z, etc.
- Number of distinct elements in set A is represented by $n(A)$. Similarly, $n(B)$, $n(C)$, $n(X)$, $n(Y)$, $n(Z)$, etc. represent number of distinct elements in sets B, C, X, Y, Z, etc., respectively.
- The symbol $\in$ represents that an element belongs to the set or that the element is present in the set.
- The symbol $\notin$ represents that an element does not belong to the set or that the element is not present in the set.
- Symbols of some sets used in mathematics:
    - (i)   **N** : the set of all natural numbers
    - (ii)   **Z** : the set of all integers
    - (iii)   **Q** : the set of all rational numbers
    - (iv)   **T** : the set of all irrational numbers
    - (v)   **R** : the set of real numbers
    - (vi) $\mathbf{Z}^+$: the set of positive integers
    - (vii) $\mathbf{Q}^+$: the set of positive rational numbers
    - (viii) $\mathbf{R}^+$: the set of positive real numbers.
    - (ix)   **C** : the set of all complex numbers

---

2 Types of Sets

    (i)   Empty Set   (ii) Singleton Set

    (ii)   Finite Set   (iv) Infinite Set

2.1 Empty Set

A set which does not contain any element is known as empty set.

- It is denoted by the symbol ϕ
- It is also represented by empty curly braces { }, i.e., $\phi = \{ \}$
- It is also known as Null or Void set.
- Number of elements in empty set $\phi = 0$

2.2 Singleton Set

A set which contains only one element is known as singleton set.

- If A is a singleton set, then $n(A) = 1$

2.3 Finite Set

A set which is empty or consists of a definite number of elements is called finite set.

- If set A is a finite set , then either $n(A) = 0$ or $n(A)$ is some natural number.
- Empty set, ϕ is also a finite set.

2.4 Infinite Set

A set which consists of indefinite (unlimited) number of elements is called infinite set.

- While writing an infinite set in roster form, only a few elements are listed in such a manner which clearly indicates the pattern in the elements, and these elements are followed by 3 dots or preceded by 3 dots.
- Set **R** of all real numbers cannot be represented in roster form because the elements of this set do not follow any particular pattern.

3 Subset

If every element of set A is also an element of set B , then A is said to be a subset of B.

- If set A is a subset of set B , then we write it as $A \subset B$.
- If set A is not a subset of set B , then we write it as $A \not\subset B$.
- If $x \in A \Rightarrow x \in B$, then $A \subset B$.
  Also, if $A \subset B$, then $x \in A \Rightarrow x \in B$.

- If $x \notin B \Rightarrow x \notin A$, then $A \subset B$.
  Also, if $A \subset B$, then $x \notin B \Rightarrow x \notin A$.

- Every set is a subset of itself, i.e., If A is any set, then $A \subset A$.
- Empty set ϕ is subset of every set.
  i.e., If A is any set , then $\phi \subset A$

- If the number of elements in set A is equal to m , then the number of its subsets is equal to 2^m.

4 *Power Set

A set of all the subsets of a given set is called as power set of that given set.

- Power set of any set A is denoted by $P(A)$.
- Every element of a power set is a set. So usually, its elements are represented by capital letters instead of small letters.
  e.g., we write $X \in P(A)$ instead of $x \in P(A)$.

- If the number of elements in set A is equal to m , then the number of its subsets is equal to 2^m.
  $\therefore$ if $\quad n(A) = m$, $\qquad$ then $\qquad n[P(A)] = 2^m$

5 Equal and Unequal sets

Two sets are said to be equal if they contain exactly the same elements. Otherwise, the sets are said to be unequal.

- If every element of set A is also an element of set B, and every element of set B is also an element of set A, then the sets A and B are said to be equal.
- For equal set A and B, we write $A = B$.
- For unequal sets A and B, we write $A \neq B$.
- If $A \subset B$ and $B \subset A$, then $A = B$.
  Also, if $A = B$, then $A \subset B$ and $B \subset A$.

6   Proper Subset and Superset

If every element of set A is also an element of set B, but every element of set B is not an element of set A, then the sets A is called as proper subset of B.

Also, B is said to be superset of A.

- If $A \subset B$ but $A \neq B$, then A is known as proper subset of B. Also, B is said to be superset of A.

7   Equivalent Sets

Two sets are said to be equivalent if they contain the same number of elements.

- If $n(A) = n(B)$, then A and B are equivalent sets.

8   Intervals: Subsets of set R of Real Numbers

(i)   The set of all the numbers lying between two real numbers a and b is an *open interval* and is denoted by (a,b). This interval does not contain end points a and b.
  - Thus, $(a,b) = \{ x : x \in \mathbf{R} \text{ and } a < x < b \}$

(ii)   The set of all the numbers from the real number a to number b which also contains end points a and b is called *closed interval* and is denoted by $[a,b]$.
  - Thus, $[a,b] = \{ x : x \in \mathbf{R} \text{ and } a \leq x \leq b \}$

(iii)   The set of all the numbers from the real number a to number b which does not contain a but contains b is an *open interval* and is denoted by $(a,b]$.
  - Thus, $(a,b] = \{ x : x \in \mathbf{R} \text{ and } a < x \leq b \}$

(iv)   The set of all the numbers from the real number a to number b which contains a but not b is *open interval* and is denoted by $[a,b)$.
  - Thus, $[a,b) = \{ x : x \in \mathbf{R} \text{ and } a \leq x < b \}$

- The set $[\, 0, \infty)$ defines the set of non-negative real numbers, while set $(-\infty, 0\,)$ defines the set of negative real numbers. The set $(-\infty, \infty\,)$ describes the set of all real numbers.
- The number $(b - a)$ is called the length of any of the intervals $(a,\, b)$, $[a,\, b]$, $[a,\, b)$ or $(a,\, b]$.

---

9   Universal Set

A set which contains all the elements of all the sets in the given context is called as universal set.

- All the possible sets in a given context are subsets of the universal set.
- The universal set is usually denoted by U.

10   Venn Diagram

- The universal set is represented usually by a rectangle.
- All other sets are represented by closed curves, usually circles in the rectangle of universal set.
- Elements of sets are written in their respective circles

11   Operations on Sets

(i) Union of sets

(ii) Intersection of sets

(iii) Difference of sets

(iv) Complement of set

11.1   Union of sets

The set containing all those elements which are present in either set A or set B or both sets A and B is called as union of sets A and B. We write it as $A \cup B$.

- $A \cup B = \{ x : x \in A \text{ or } x \in B \}$

Venn Diagram

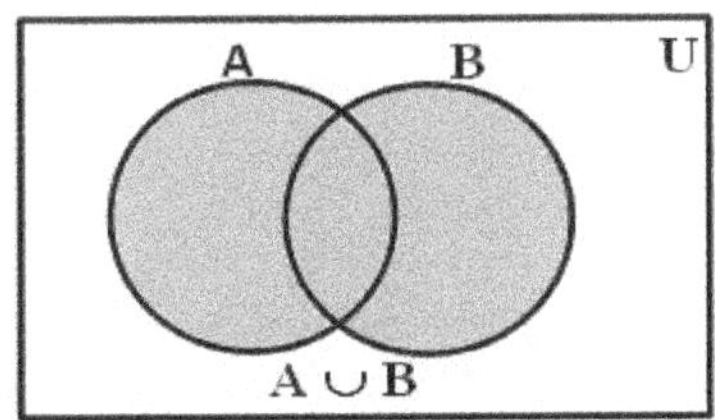

Properties of Union of sets:

(i)   Commutative Law: $A \cup B = B \cup A$

(ii)   Associative Law : $(A \cup B) \cup C = A \cup (B \cup C)$

(iii)   Law of identity: Identity element of $\cup$ is ϕ .

$$\text{i.e.,} \quad A \cup \phi = A = \phi \cup A$$

(iv) Idempotent Law: $A \cup A = A$

(v) Law of **U** : $A \cup U = U$

11.2 Intersection of sets

The set containing all those elements which are present in both sets A and B is called as intersection of sets A and B. We write it as $A \cap B$.

- $A \cap B = \{ x : x \in A \text{ and } x \in B \}$

Venn Diagram

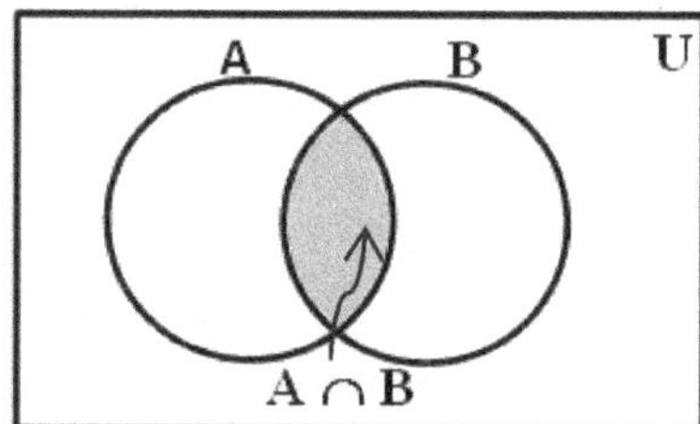

Properties of Intersection of sets:

(i) Commutative Law: $A \cap B = B \cap A$

(ii) Associative Law : $(A \cap B) \cap C = A \cap (B \cap C)$

(iii) Law of identity: Identity element of $\cap$ is **U**.

$$\text{i.e.,} \quad A \cap U = A = U \cap A$$

(iv) Idempotent Law: $A \cap A = A$

(v) Law of ϕ : $A \cap \phi = \phi$

- Distributive Law:
  (i) $\cup$ is distributive over $\cap$: $A \cup (B \cap C) = (A \cup B) \cap (A \cup C)$
  (ii) $\cap$ is distributive over $\cup$: $A \cap (B \cup C) = (A \cap B) \cup (A \cap C)$
- Disjoint Sets:
  If $A \cap B = \phi$, then A and B are known as *Disjoint Sets*.

Disjoint Sets
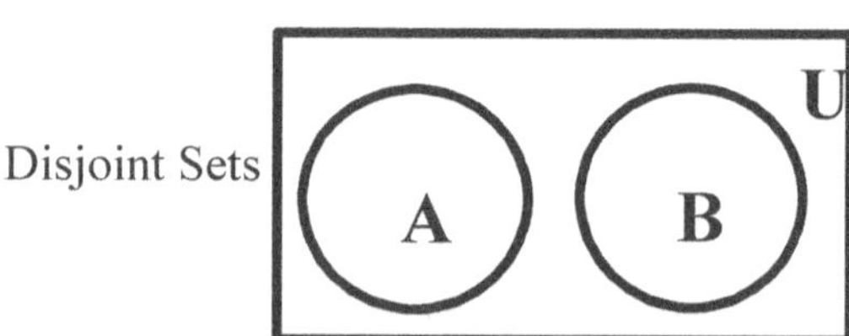

11.3 Difference of sets

The set of all those elements which belong to set A but do not belong to set B is difference of A and B. We write it as A – B.

- A – B = { $x : x \in$ A and $x \notin$ B }

Venn Diagram

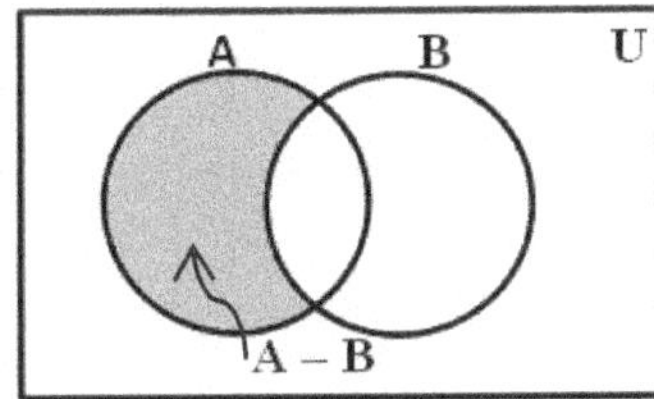

11.4 Complement of set

The set containing all those elements of universal set U which are not present in set A is called as complement of set A. We write it as A′ or A^c .

- A′ = { $x : x \in$ U and $x \notin$ A }
- A′ = U – A.

Venn Diagram

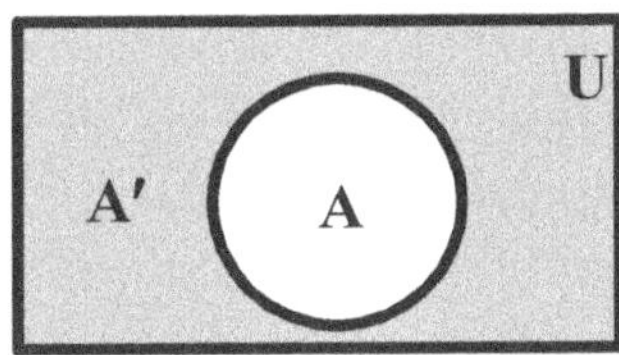

- A – B = A $\cap$ B′

Properties of Complement of set:

(i)   (A′)′ = A
(ii)   A $\cup$ A′ = U
(iii)   A $\cap$ A′ = ϕ
(iv) ϕ′ = U
(v)   U′ = ϕ

De Morgan's Law:

(i)   (A $\cup$ B)′ = A′ $\cap$ B′

(ii)   (A $\cap$ B)′ = A′ $\cup$ B′

---

12 *Formulae for 2 sets

Let   U is universal set. A and B are 2 subsets of **U**.

- Number of elements in 'set A or set B' (in at least one of the 2 sets):
$$n(A \cup B) = n(A) + n(B) - n(A \cap B)$$

- Number of elements in 'only set A' (in set 'A but not in B') :
$$n(A - B) = n(A) - n(A \cap B)$$

- Number of elements in 'only set B' (in set 'B but not in A'):
$$n(B - A) = n(B) - n(A \cap B)$$

- Number of elements in 'neither set A nor set B':
$$n(A' \cap B') = n(A \cup B)'$$
$$= n(U) - n(A \cup B)$$

13 *Formulae for 3 sets

Let   **U** = universal set.   A, B and C are 3 subsets of **U**.

- Number of elements in 'set A or set B or set C' (in at least one of the 3 sets):
$$n(A \cup B \cup C) = n(A) + n(B) + n(C) - n(A \cap B) - n(B \cap C) - n(C \cap A) + n(A \cap B \cap C)$$

- Number of elements in 'only set A' (in set 'A but neither in B nor in C') $= n(A) - n(A \cap B) - n(C \cap A) + n(A \cap B \cap C)$
- Number of elements in 'only set B' (in set 'B but neither in A nor in C') $= n(B) - n(A \cap B) - n(B \cap C) + n(A \cap B \cap C)$
- Number of elements in 'only set C' (in set 'C but neither in B nor in A') $= n(C) - n(C \cap A) - n(B \cap C) + n(A \cap B \cap C)$
- Number of elements in exactly one set
$$= n(A) + n(B) + n(C) - 2\,[n(A \cap B) + n(B \cap C) + n(C \cap A)] + 3\,[n(A \cap B \cap C)]$$

- Number of elements in set 'A and B but not in C'
$$= n(A \cap B) - n(A \cap B \cap C)$$

- Number of elements in set 'B and C but not in A'
$$= n(B \cap C) - n(A \cap B \cap C)$$

- Number of elements in set 'C and A but not in B'
$$= n(C \cap A) - n(A \cap B \cap C)$$

- Number of elements in 'exactly two sets'
$$= n(A \cap B) + n(B \cap C) + n(C \cap A) - 3\,[n(A \cap B \cap C)]$$

- Number of elements which are 'not in any of the 3 sets':
$$n(A' \cap B' \cap C') = n(A \cup B \cup C)'$$
$$= n(U) - n(A \cup B \cup C)$$

14 Important Concepts

If an element belongs to a certain set, then we draw some conclusions from it as follows:

- $x \in A \cup B \Rightarrow x \in A$ or $x \in B$
- $x \in A \cup B$ does not imply that $x \in A$
- $x \in A \Rightarrow x \in A \cup B$

- $x \in A \cap B \Rightarrow x \in A$ and $x \in B$
- $x \in A \cap B \Rightarrow x \in A$
- $x \in A$ does not imply that $x \in A \cap B$

- $x \in A \Rightarrow x \notin A'$
- $x \in A' \Rightarrow x \notin A$
- $x \notin A \Rightarrow x \in A'$
- $x \notin A' \Rightarrow x \in A$

- $x \in A - B \Rightarrow x \in A$ and $x \notin B$
- $x \in A - B \Rightarrow x \in A$ and $x \in B'$
- $x \in A - B \Rightarrow x \in A \cap B'$
- $x \in A \cap B' \Rightarrow x \in A - B$

- If $A \subset B$, then
  (i) $x \in A \Rightarrow x \in B$
  (ii) $x \notin A$ does not imply that $x \notin B$
  (iii) $x \notin B \Rightarrow x \notin A$
  (iv) $x \in B$ does not imply that $x \in A$
  (v) $A \cap B = A$
  (vi) $A \cup B = B$

- $x \in A \Rightarrow \{\,x\,\} \in P(A)$
- $X \subset A \Rightarrow X \in P(A)$
  $X \in P(A) \Rightarrow X \subset A$

Chapter-2   Relations and Functions

1 Ordered pair

Two elements grouped together in a particular order, represent an ordered pair.

- If a and b are two elements , then (a, b) or (b, a) represent an ordered pair.
- Two ordered pairs are equal if and only if first element of one pair is equal to the first of other, and second element is equal to the second of the other.

  i.e., If $(a, b) = (c, d)$, then $a = c$ and $b = d$.

  Also, if $a = c$ and $b = d$, then $(a, b) = (c, d)$
- For different elements a & b : $(a, b) \neq (b, a)$

2 Ordered triplet

Three elements grouped together in a particular order, represent an ordered triplet.

- If a, b and c are three elements , then (a, b, c) represent an ordered triplet.
- Two ordered triplets are equal if and only if their corresponding first, second and third elements are equal.

3 Cartesian Product

The set of all ordered pairs of elements from 2 non-empty sets A and B is called as Cartesian Product $A \times B$.

i.e., $A \times B = \{ (a,b) : a \in A, b \in B \}$

Also, $B \times A = \{ (b,a) : a \in A, b \in B \}$

- If either of the sets A or B is empty , then A x B is also empty.

  i.e., If $A = \phi$ or $B = \phi$, then $A \times B = \phi$
- For different sets A and B, $A \times B \neq B \times A$
- If there are p elements in set A and q elements in set B, then there will be pq elements in $A \times B$.

  i.e., if $n(A) = p$ and $n(B) = q$, then $n(A \times B) = pq$.

- Cartesian product of three sets:
  $A \times B \times C = \{ (a,b,c) : a \in A, b \in B, c \in C \}$
- We can also have Cartesian product $A \times A$
  $$A \times A = \{ (a,b) : a \in A, b \in A \}$$

  Also, $A \times A \times A = \{ (a,b,c) : a \in A, b \in A, c \in A \}$

4 Relation

Any subset of $A \times B$ is a relation from set A to set B.

- In every ordered pair of a relation, first element is said to be related with the second element.
- Second element of an ordered pair is called as the *image* of the first element.
- The total number of relations that can be defined from a set A to a set B is the number of possible subsets of $A \times B$.
  i.e., If $n(A) = p$ and $n(B) = q$, then $n(A \times B) = pq$ and
  The total number of relations $= 2^{pq}$.
- A relation from set A to set A is also stated as relation on set A.

4.1 Domain

The set of first elements of all the ordered pairs in relation R from set A to set B is called the *domain* of the relation R.

4.2 Range

The set of second elements of all the ordered pairs in relation R from set A to set B is called the *range* of the relation R.

4.3 Codomain

The whole set B is called the *codomain* of the relation R.

- Range $\subseteq$ Codomain.

4.4 Arrow Diagram

An arrow diagram is a visual representation of a relation R from set A to set B in which an arrow is drawn from an element in set A to its image in set B under the given relation.

For example, if relation $R : A \rightarrow B$ is defined as
$R = \{(1, b), (2, d), (4, c)\}$, where $A = \{1,2,3,4,5\}$ and
$B = \{a, b, c, d, e, f, \}$, then its arrow diagram is as shown.

---

*Asterisk (*) marked article (if any) is **not** in CBSE 2025-26 syllabus.*

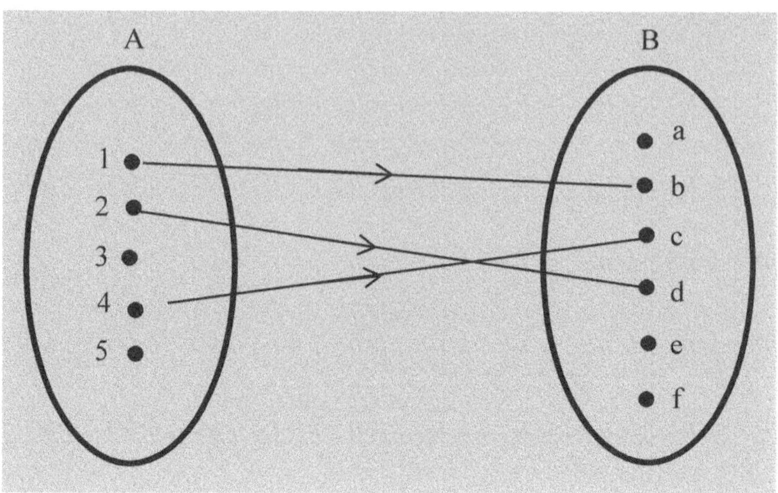

5   Function

If every element of set A has one and only one image in set B under the given relation , then the relation is known as a function from set A to set B.

- If f is a function from A to B , we write it as $f : A \to B$.
- If $(a, b) \in f$, then $f(a) = b$, where b is called the *image* of a under f, *and* a is called the *pre-image* of b under f.
- Every function is relation, but every relation is not function.

5.1 Real Valued Function

If the range of a function is set of real numbers or one of its subsets , then the function is known as a *Real Valued Function*.

i.e., If Range $\subseteq$ **R,** then function is a real valued function.

5.2 Real Function

If the domain and range of a function are both sets of real numbers or any subsets of real numbers , then the function is known as a *Real Function*.

i.e., If Domain $\subseteq$ **R** and Range $\subseteq$ **R** , function is a real function.

---

6 Some Important Functions

6.1 Identity Function

The function $f: \mathbf{R} \to \mathbf{R}$ defined by $f(x) = x$ is called as *Identity Function*.

(Remember $\mathbf{R}$ is set of real numbers)

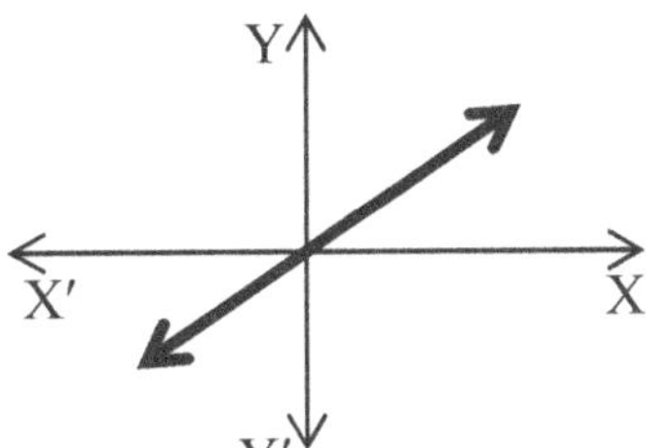

- Domain = $\mathbf{R}$
- Range = $\mathbf{R}$

6.2 Constant Function

A function $f: \mathbf{R} \to \mathbf{R}$ defined by $f(x) = k$, where $k \in \mathbf{R}$, is called as *Constant Function*.

e.g. $f(x) = 2$

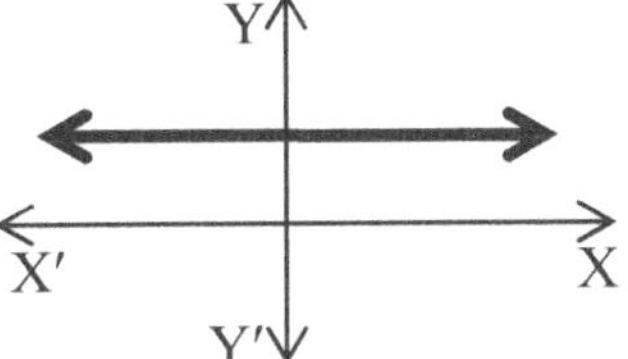

- Domain = $\mathbf{R}$
- Range = $\{\,k\,\}$

6.3 Polynomial Functions

A function $f: \mathbf{R} \to \mathbf{R}$ defined by $f(x) = a_0 + a_1 x + a_2 x^2 + a_3 x^3 + \ldots + a_n x^n$, where n is a non-negative integer, and a_0, a_1, a_2, a_3, ..., $a_n \in \mathbf{R}$ is called as *Polynomial Function*.

- Domain = $\mathbf{R}$ and Range varies
- Constant function is also a polynomial function with degree = 0
- Identity function is also a polynomial function with degree = 1

6.3.1 Linear Polynomial Function

A function $f: \mathbf{R} \to \mathbf{R}$ defined by $f(x) = a\,x + b$

where $a, b \in \mathbf{R}$ and $a \neq 0$ is called as *Linear Function*.

---

*Asterisk (*) marked article (if any) is **not** in CBSE 2025-26 syllabus.*

- A polynomial function of degree 1 is called as linear function.
- Domain = **R** and Range = **R**
- Graph is a **straight line** inclined to axes.
- Identity function is also a linear function.

6.3.2 Quadratic Polynomial Function

A function $f : \mathbf{R} \to \mathbf{R}$ defined by $f(x) = a\,x^2 + b\,x + c$, where $a, b, c \in \mathbf{R}$ and $a \neq 0$ is called as *Quadratic Function*.

- A polynomial function of degree 2 is called as quadratic function.
- Domain = **R** and Range varies
- Graph is a **parabola** with its axis of symmetry as Y-axis or parallel to Y-axis.

6.3.3 Cubic Polynomial Function

A function $f : \mathbf{R} \to \mathbf{R}$ defined by $f(x) = a\,x^3 + b\,x^2 + c\,x + d$, where $a, b, c, d \in \mathbf{R}$ and $a \neq 0$ is called as *Cubic Function*.

- A polynomial function of degree 3 is called as cubic function.
- Domain = **R** and Range = **R**

6.4 Rational Function

A *Rational Function* is a function $f : \mathbf{A} \to \mathbf{R}$ defined by

$$f(x) = \frac{h(x)}{g(x)}$$, where $h(x)$ and $g(x)$ both are polynomial functions, and the domain **A** of $f(x)$ is such that $g(x) \neq 0$.

- Domain and Range vary from function to function (i.e, not same for all rational functions)
- Reciprocal function $f(x) = \dfrac{1}{x}$, $x \neq 0$ is also a rational function.

6.5 Modulus Function

The function $f : \mathbf{R} \to \mathbf{R}$ defined by $f(x) = |x|$ is called as *Modulus Function*.

It means $f(x) = \begin{cases} x, & x \geq 0 \\ -x, & x < 0 \end{cases}$

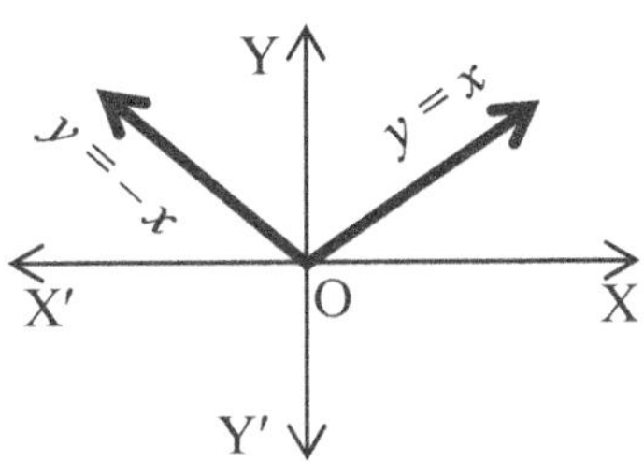

- Domain = **R**
- Range = $[\,0, \infty\,)$

6.6 Signum Function

Signum Function is the function $f : \mathbf{R} \to \mathbf{R}$ defined by

$$f(x) = \begin{cases} 1, & x > 0 \\ 0, & x = 0 \\ -1, & x < 0 \end{cases}$$

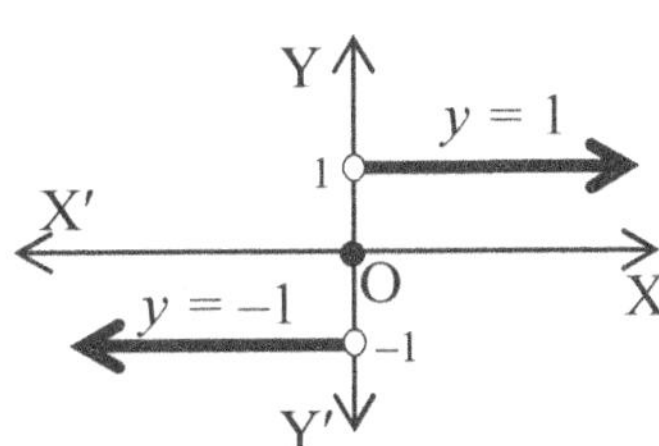

- Domain = **R**
- Range = $\{\,-1, 0, 1\,\}$

6.7 Greatest Integer Function

The function $f : \mathbf{R} \to \mathbf{R}$ written as $f(x) = [\,x\,]$, which gives the value of greatest integer less than or equal to x is called *Greatest Integer Function*.

It means

$[x] = -2$ for $-2 \leq x < -1$

$[x] = -1$ for $-1 \leq x < 0$

$[x] = 0 \quad$ for $0 \leq x < 1$

$[x] = 1 \quad$ for $1 \leq x < 2$

$[x] = 2 \quad$ for $2 \leq x < 3$

$\qquad$ and so on

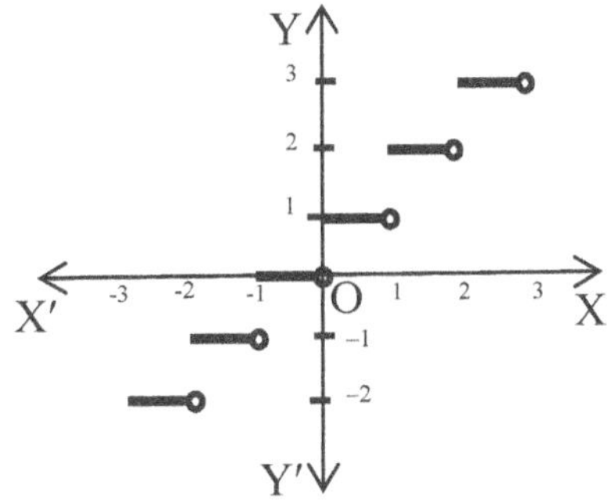

- Domain = **R**
- Range = **Z**
  (Remember **Z** is set of integers)

---

*Asterisk (*) marked article (if any) is **not** in CBSE 2025-26 syllabus.*

7   Algebra of Real Functions

Let $f : X \to \mathbf{R}$ and $g : X \to \mathbf{R}$ be any two real functions,

where $X \subset \mathbf{R}$. Their addition, subtraction, multiplication and division are defined as follows:

7.1   Addition

$(f + g) : X \to \mathbf{R}$ is a function such that

$$(f + g)(x) = f(x) + g(x) \text{ for all } x \in X$$

7.2   Subtraction

$(f - g) : X \to \mathbf{R}$ is a function such that

$$(f - g)(x) = f(x) - g(x) \text{ for all } x \in X$$

7.3   Multiplication

$fg : X \to \mathbf{R}$ is a function such that

$$(fg)(x) = f(x)\, g(x) \text{ for all } x \in X$$

7.4   Division

$\dfrac{f}{g}$ is a function such that

$$\left(\frac{f}{g}\right)(x) = \frac{f(x)}{g(x)} \text{ provided } g(x) \neq 0 \text{ and } x \in X$$

- Domain of the function obtained after addition, subtraction, and multiplication remains same as the common domain of the added functions f and g. But domain of the function obtained after division may or may not be same as the common domain.

Chapter-3   Trigonometry

---

1 **(i)** $1° = \frac{\pi}{180} \, rad$ **(ii)** $1 \, rad = \frac{180}{\pi} \, degree$

2 **Arc Length**

$arc \ length = radius \times angle \ in \ radian$

$$l = r \, \theta$$

3 **Basic Formulae**

(i) $sin^2\theta + cos^2\theta = 1$

(ii) $sec^2\theta - tan^2\theta = 1$

(iii) $cosec^2\theta - cot^2\theta = 1$

4 **Sum and Difference of Angles**

(i) $sin(A + B) = sinAcosB + cosAsinB$

(ii) $sin(A - B) = sinAcosB - cosAsinB$

(iii) $cos(A + B) = cosAcosB - sinAsinB$

(iv) $cos(A - B) = cosAcosB + sinAsinB$

(v) $tan(A + B) = \dfrac{tanA + tanB}{1 - tanA \, tanB}$

(vi) $tan(A - B) = \dfrac{tanA - tanB}{1 + tanA \, tanB}$

(vii) $cot(A + B) = \dfrac{cotA \, cotB - 1}{cotB + cotA}$

$(viii)$ $cot(A - B) = \dfrac{cotA \, cotB + 1}{cotB - cotA}$

---

5   Double Angle Formulae

(i) $\sin 2A = 2\sin A\cos A$

(ii) $\sin 2A = \dfrac{2\tan A}{1+\tan^2 A}$

(iii) $\cos 2A = \cos^2 A - \sin^2 A$

(iv) $\cos 2A = 1 - 2\sin^2 A$

(v) $\cos 2A = 2\cos^2 A - 1$

(vi) $\cos 2A = \dfrac{1-\tan^2 A}{1+\tan^2 A}$

(vii) $\tan 2A = \dfrac{2\tan A}{1-\tan^2 A}$

6   Triple Angle Formulae

(i) $\sin 3A = 3\sin A - 4\sin^3 A$

(ii) $\cos 3A = 4\cos^3 A - 3\cos A$

(iii) $\tan 3A = \dfrac{3\tan A - \tan^3 A}{1 - 3\tan^2 A}$

7   Half Angle Formulae

(i) $2\sin^2 \dfrac{A}{2} = 1 - \cos A \;\Rightarrow\; \sin \dfrac{A}{2} = \pm\sqrt{\dfrac{1-\cos A}{2}}$

(ii) $2\cos^2 \dfrac{A}{2} = 1 + \cos A \;\Rightarrow\; \cos \dfrac{A}{2} = \pm\sqrt{\dfrac{1+\cos A}{2}}$

(iii) $\tan^2 \dfrac{A}{2} = \dfrac{1-\cos A}{1+\cos A} \;\Rightarrow\; \tan \dfrac{A}{2} = \pm\sqrt{\dfrac{1-\cos A}{1+\cos A}}$

8   Ratio Sum or Difference Formulae

(i) $sinA + sinB = 2sin\dfrac{A+B}{2} . cos\dfrac{A-B}{2}$

(ii) $sinA - sinB = 2sin\dfrac{A-B}{2} . cos\dfrac{A+B}{2}$

(iii) $cosA + cosB = 2cos\dfrac{A+B}{2} . cos\dfrac{A-B}{2}$

(iv) $cosA - cosB = -2sin\dfrac{A+B}{2} . sin\dfrac{A-B}{2}$

9   Product Formulae

(i) $2sinAcosB = \sin(A + B) + \sin(A - B)$

(ii) $2cosAsinB = \sin(A + B) - \sin(A - B)$

(iii) $2cosAcosB = \cos(A + B) + \cos(A - B)$

(iv) $2sinAsinB = \cos(A - B) - \cos(A + B)$

10 More formulae

(i) $sin^2A - sin^2B = \sin(A + B)\sin(A - B)$

(ii) $cos^2A - sin^2B = \cos(A + B)\cos(A - B)$

(iii) $1 - cosA = 2sin^2\dfrac{A}{2}$

(iv) $1 + cosA = 2cos^2\dfrac{A}{2}$

11 Domain and Range

S.N.	Functions	Domain	Range
1)	$y = sin\ x$	$\mathbf{R}$ *i.e.,* $-\infty < x < \infty$	$[-1, 1]$ *i.e.,* $-1 \le y \le 1$
2)	$y = cos\ x$	$\mathbf{R}$ *i.e.,* $-\infty < x < \infty$	$[-1, 1]$ *i.e.,* $-1 \le y \le 1$
3)	$y = tan\ x$	$\mathbf{R} - \{(2n+1)\frac{\pi}{2}\}$	$\mathbf{R}$ *i.e.,* $-\infty < y < \infty$
4)	$y = cosec\ x$	$\mathbf{R} - \{n\pi\}$	$\mathbf{R} - (-1, 1)$ *i.e.,* $y \le -1\ or\ y \ge 1$
5)	$y = sec\ x$	$\mathbf{R} - \{(2n+1)\frac{\pi}{2}\}$	$\mathbf{R} - (-1, 1)$ *i.e.,* $y \le -1\ or\ y \ge 1$
6)	$y = cot\ x$	$\mathbf{R} - \{n\pi\}$	$\mathbf{R}$ *i.e.,* $-\infty < y < \infty$

- *Note:* **R** *denotes set of real numbers in the above table.*

*Asterisk (*) marked article (if any) is **not** in CBSE 2025-26 syllabus.*

12 *General Solutions of Trigonometric Equations

(i) If $\sin\theta = 0$,
then $\theta = n\pi$ where $n \in Z$

(ii) If $\cos\theta = 0$,

then $\theta = (2n+1)\dfrac{\pi}{2}$ where $n \in Z$

(iii) If $\tan\theta = 0$,
then $\theta = n\pi$ where $n \in Z$

(iv) If $\sin\theta = \sin\alpha$,
then $\theta = n\pi + (-1)^n \alpha$ where $n \in Z$

(v) If $\cos\theta = \cos\alpha$,
then $\theta = 2n\pi \pm \alpha$ where $n \in Z$

(vi) If $\tan\theta = \tan\alpha$,
then $\theta = n\pi + \alpha$ where $n \in Z$

13 *Law of Sines (sine rule)

$$\frac{a}{\sin A} = \frac{b}{\sin B} = \frac{c}{\sin C}$$

14 *Law of Cosines (cosine rule)

(i) $\cos A = \dfrac{b^2 + c^2 - a^2}{2bc}$

OR $a^2 = b^2 + c^2 - 2bc.\cos A$

(ii) $\cos B = \dfrac{c^2 + a^2 - b^2}{2ca}$

OR $b^2 = c^2 + a^2 - 2\,ca.\cos B$

(iii) $\cos C = \dfrac{a^2 + b^2 - c^2}{2ab}$

OR $c^2 = a^2 + b^2 - 2ab.\cos C$

---

*Asterisk (*) marked article (if any) is **not** in CBSE 2025-26 syllabus.*

Chapter-4   *Principle Of Mathematical Induction

1   *The Principle of Mathematical Induction

If there is a given statement P(n) involving the natural number n such that

(i)   The statement is true for n = 1,

    i.e., P(1) is true, and

(ii) If the statement is true for n = k (where k is some positive integer), then the statement is also true for n = k + 1,

    i.e., truth of P(k) implies the truth of P (k + 1).

Then, P(n) is true for all natural numbers n.

- Property (i) is simply a statement of fact. We have to verify the given statement $P(n)$ by putting value of $n = 1$.
  There may be situations when a statement is not true for some initial positive integers, but it is true for all $n \geq a$. In this case, we have to verify the given statement $P(n)$ by putting, $n = a$.

- Property (ii) is a conditional property. It does not verify or affirm that the given statement is true for $n = k$. We have to just assume that P(k) is true.

- The assumption that the given statement is true for $n = k$ is called the *inductive hypothesis*.

- Property (i) is *Basic step*, and Property (ii) is *Inductive step* .

2   *Steps in using Principle of Mathematical Induction

Step 1: Basic step

Verify the given statement $P(n)$ by putting value $n = 1$.

i.e., verify that P(1) is true.

- If P(n) is stated for $n \geq a$, then verify that P(a) is true by putting the value $n = a$.

<u>**Step 2**</u>: **Inductive step**

(i) Assume that P(k) is true , where $k \in$ **N**. (Remember **N** is set of natural numbers)

Put $n = k$ in the statement P(n).

(ii) Using the statement P(k), prove that P($k + 1$) is true.

∴ We write P($k + 1$) is true whenever P(k) is true.

By Principle of Mathematical Induction P(n) is true for all $n \in$ **N**.

Chapter-5   Complex Numbers

1   The imaginary number, i

- $\sqrt{-1} = i$ It is called iota
- $i^2 = -1,$ $i^3 = -i,$ $i^4 = 1$
- For any integer k,
  $$i^{4k} = 1, \quad i^{4k+1} = i, \quad i^{4k+2} = -1, \quad i^{4k+3} = -i$$

2   Important concept

- $\sqrt{a\,b} = \sqrt{a}\,\sqrt{b}$ only if, at least one of a and b is a positive real number.
- If both a and b are negative real numbers , then this relation does not hold.

3   Complex number, $a + i\,b$

- A number of the form $z = a + i\,b$, where $a,\ b \in \mathbf{R}$ is called a complex number.
- a is called the real part of z, denoted by $\mathrm{Re}(z)$, and b is called the imaginary part of z, denoted by $\mathrm{Im}(z)$.
  So, we write, $\mathrm{Re}(z) = a$ and $\mathrm{Im}(z) = b$.

4   Equality of Complex Numbers

- Two complex numbers are equal if and only if their real parts are equal, and their imaginary parts are equal.
  It means if $a + i\,b = c + i\,d$, then $a = c$ and $b = d$
  Also, if $a = c$ and $b = d$ then $a + i\,b = c + i\,d$

5   Comparison of Complex Numbers

- Two complex numbers having non-zero imaginary part cannot be compared.
  It means if $z_1 = a + i\,b$ and $z_2 = c + i\,d$ such that either $b \neq 0$ or $d \neq 0$, then we cannot say that one $z_2 > z_1$ or $z_1 > z_2$.
- However, if both complex numbers are purely real (i.e., $b = d = 0$),

  then we can say $z_2 > z_1$ if $c > a$ and $z_1 > z_2$ if $a > c$

---

6   Addition of Complex Numbers

- If $z_1 = a + i\,b$ and $z_2 = c + i\,d$ are 2 complex numbers, then their sum is a complex number
$$z_1 + z_2 = a + c + i\,(b + d)$$

- $\text{Re}(z_1 + z_2) = \text{Re}(z_1) + \text{Re}(z_2)$
and $\text{Im}(z_1 + z_2) = \text{Im}(z_1) + \text{Im}(z_2)$

6.1   Properties of Addition

(i) *The closure law:* The sum of two complex numbers is a complex number.

(ii) *The commutative law:* $z_1 + z_2 = z_2 + z_1$.

(iii) *The associative law:* $(z_1 + z_2) + z_3 = z_1 + (z_2 + z_3)$.

(iv) *The existence of additive identity:*
There exists complex number 'zero', $0 = 0 + i\,0$ such that, for every complex number z, $z + 0 = z$.
0 is called the additive identity of complex numbers.

(v) *The existence of additive inverse:*
For every complex number $z = a + ib$, we have the complex number $-z = -a + i(-b)$, such that $z + (-z) = 0$.
$-z$ is called the additive inverse of z or negative of z.

7   Difference of Complex Numbers

- If $z_1 = a + i\,b$ and $z_2 = c + i\,d$ are 2 complex numbers, then their difference is a complex number
$$z_1 - z_2 = a - c + i\,(b - d)$$

- $\text{Re}(z_1 - z_2) = \text{Re}(z_1) - \text{Re}(z_2)$

- $\text{Im}(z_1 - z_2) = \text{Im}(z_1) - \text{Im}(z_2)$

8   Multiplication of Complex Numbers

- If $z_1 = a + i\,b$ and $z_2 = c + i\,d$ are 2 complex numbers, then their multiplication is a complex number
$$z_1 z_2 = (a\,c - b\,d) + i(ad + bc)$$

- $\text{Re}(z_1 z_2) = \text{Re}(z_1).\text{Re}(z_2) - \text{Im}(z_1).\text{Im}(z_2)$

- $\text{Im}(z_1 z_2) = \text{Re}(z_1)\,\text{Im}(z_2) + \text{Re}(z_2)\,\text{Im}(z_1)$

8.1 Properties of Multiplication

(i) *The closure law:* The multiplication of two complex numbers is a complex number.

(ii) *The commutative law:* $z_1 z_2 = z_2 z_1$.

(iii) *The associative law:* $(z_1 z_2) z_3 = z_1 (z_2 z_3)$.

(iv) *The existence of multiplicative identity*:

There exists the complex number $1 = 1 + i\,0$ such that,

for every complex number z, $z.1 = z$.

1 is called multiplicative identity of complex numbers.

(v) *The existence of multiplicative inverse*:

For every non-zero complex number $z = a + ib$, we have

the complex number $\dfrac{1}{z}$ such that $\dfrac{1}{z}.z = 1$.

$\dfrac{1}{z}$ **is multiplicative inverse of z.**

9 Conjugate of Complex Number, $\bar{z}$

- If $z = a + ib$, then its conjugate is $\bar{z} = \overline{a + ib} = a - ib$
  It means sign of imaginary part is changed to get the conjugate of a complex number.

10 Modulus of Complex Number, $|z|$

If $z = a + ib$, then its modulus is $|z| = |a + ib| = \sqrt{a^2 + b^2}$

11 Other Results and formulae

- $|z| = |\bar{z}|$

- $\dfrac{1}{z} = \dfrac{\bar{z}}{|z|^2}$

- $z\,\bar{z} = |z|^2$

- $\overline{(z_1 + z_2)} = \overline{z_1} + \overline{z_2}$ and $\overline{(z_1 - z_2)} = \overline{z_1} - \overline{z_2}$

- $\overline{z_1 z_2} = \overline{z_1} . \overline{z_2}$

- $\overline{\left(\dfrac{z_1}{z_2}\right)} = \dfrac{\overline{z_1}}{\overline{z_2}}$

- $|z_1 z_2| = |z_1||z_2|$ and $\left|\dfrac{z_1}{z_2}\right| = \dfrac{|z_1|}{|z_2|}$

- $|z_1 + z_2| \le |z_1| + |z_2|$ and $|z_1 - z_2| \ge \big||z_1| - |z_2|\big|$

12 Argand Plane and Polar Form

- A complex number can be represented on a plane just like a point on a cartesian plane. The Cartesian plane on which every point represents a unique complex number is called **Complex plane or Argand Plane.**

- On this plane, Real part of the complex number is represented on X-axis and imaginary part on Y-axis. So, X-axis is known as real axis and Y-axis as imaginary axis (see figure below).

- In the figure below,
  point A denotes a complex number $z = x + i\,y$.

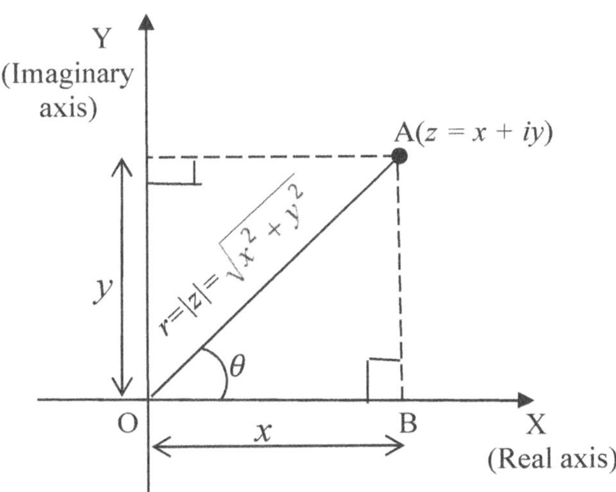

- Length of the line segment joining origin O with the point A denotes **modulus 'r'** of the complex number.
- Angle made by OA with positive direction of X-axis is known as *argument of z* and is written as *arg z*. In the figure $\theta = arg\ z$. It is also called as *amplitude* of z.
- Principal argument of a complex number is taken such that $-\pi < \theta \le \pi$
- From the figure, we can easily see that

$$x = r\,cos\theta \text{ and } y = r\,sin\theta.$$

So, we can write the complex number as

$$z = r\,(\,cos\theta + i\,sin\theta\,).$$

This is known as **Polar Form** of the complex number.

13 *Converting a complex number into Polar Form

For the given complex no. $z = (...) + i\,(...\,)$
Note down the real part as $x = ...$
and Imaginary part as $y = ...$
Calculate the modulus of z as $r = \sqrt{x^2 + y^2}$
Now let argument of z be θ.

$$\therefore tan\,\theta \;=\; \frac{y}{x}\,.$$

Find acute angle α such that $tan\,\alpha \;=\; \left|\frac{y}{x}\right|$

Now check the quadrant of z by locating the coordinates (x,y) in the Cartesian system.

Take $\theta = \alpha$ if z lies in Ist quadrant
Take $\theta = \pi - \alpha$ if z lies in IInd quadrant
Take $\theta = -\,\pi + \alpha$ if z lies in IIIrd quadrant
Take $\theta = -\,\alpha$ if z lies in IVth quadrant

Now write the complex number in polar form as
$z = r\,(\,cos\theta + i\,sin\theta\,)$ by putting values of r and θ found above in it.

Chapter-6   Linear Inequalities

1   Inequality and its kinds

Two real numbers or two algebraic expressions related by the symbol '$<$', '$>$', '$\leq$' or '$\geq$' form an *inequality*.

(i)   **Numerical Inequality:** Two real numbers related by the symbol '$<$', '$>$', '$\leq$' or '$\geq$' form a *numerical inequality*.

(ii)   **Literal Inequality:** Two algebraic expressions related by the symbol '$<$', '$>$', '$\leq$' or '$\geq$' form a *literal inequality*.

(iii)   **Strict Inequality:** An inequality with symbols '$<$' or '$>$' is a *strict inequality*.

(iv)   **Slack Inequality:** An inequality with symbols '$\leq$' or '$\geq$' is a *slack inequality*.

(v)   Inequality containing one variable and having degree one is *linear inequality* in one variable.

(vi)   Inequality containing one variable and having degree two is *quadratic inequality* in one variable.

(vii)   Inequality containing two variables and having degree one is *linear inequality* in two variables.

2   Rules for solving an inequality

Rule 1 When equal numbers are added to or subtracted from both sides of an inequality, then the sign of inequality *remains same*.

Rule 2 When both sides are multiplied or divided by a positive number, then the sign of inequality *remains same*.

Rule 3 When both sides are multiplied or divided by a negative number, then the sign of inequality is *reversed*.

3   Representing solution of an inequality in one variable

- When the solution is required in the set of natural numbers or integers or whole numbers, then all the values of the required solution are listed.
- When the solution is required in the set of real numbers, then we write the solution as interval. It may be in one of forms: (a, b), $(a, b]$, $[a, b)$ or $[a, b]$

- Solutions in the intervals of real numbers can be represented on a number line as follows:
  (i) Open end of the interval is represented by a small **blank** circle.
  (ii) Closed end of the interval is represented by a small **dark** circle.

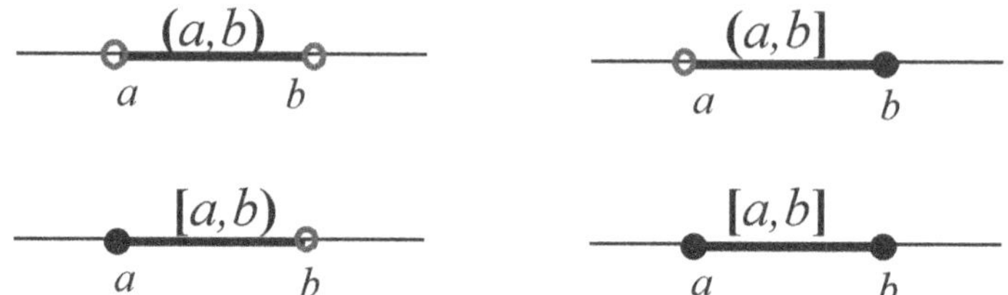

4 *Graphical solution of a Linear Inequality in two variables

The inequalities can be in any one of the following forms:

(i) $ax + by > c$ (ii) $ax + by < c$

(iii) $ax + by \geq c$ (iv) $ax + by \leq c$

We take the following steps to find solutions graphically:

Step-1 For all the above form, draw the graph of the equation:
$$ax + by = c.$$ It will be a straight line.

- If the inequality is of the form $ax + by \geq c$ or $ax + by \leq c$, then draw a **continuous line**.
- If the inequality is of the form $ax + by > c$ or $ax + by < c$, then draw a **broken or dotted line**.
- The line divides the plane into two half planes. Only one of these half planes will contain the solutions. The region containing all the solutions of an inequality is called the *solution region*.

Step-2 **(Identify the solution region)** Take any point (a, b) which does not lie on the line, and check whether it satisfies the inequality or not. For convenience, take the point $(0, 0)$ if it does not lie on the line.

- If the point satisfies the inequality, then the half plane which contains the point is the solution region. We shade that plane to represent the solution.

- If it does not satisfy the inequality, then the half plane which does not contain the point is the solution region. We shade that plane to represent the solution.

5 *Graphical solution of System of Linear Inequalities in two variables

Here, we are given two or more inequalities.

Step-1 We draw the graphs, and find the solution regions for all the individual inequalities.

Step-2 The region common to the all the above obtained regions is the required solution region of the system of linear inequalities. We shade that common region to represent required solution.

Chapter-7   Permutations And Combinations

1 Factorial

If n is any natural number, then factorial of n is product of first n natural numbers.

- $n! = n\,(n–1)\,(n–2)\,(n–3)\ldots 3.2.1$, where n is any natural number

  e.g., $5! = 5 \times 4 \times 3 \times 2 \times 1 = 120$
- $1! = 1$
- $0! = 1$

2 Fundamental Principle of Counting

If a job can be performed in m different ways, and for each such way, second job can be done in n different ways , then the two jobs (in order) can be completed in $m \times n$ ways.

For example, suppose there are 3 paths to go from place A to B and 2 paths to go from B to C.

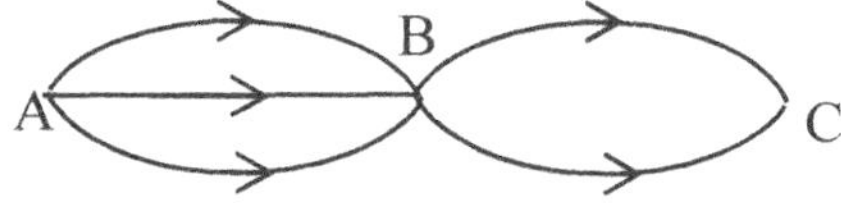

If we want to go from A to C via B , then we divide our job into two parts, i.e.,

No. of ways to go from A to B = 3 (Ist part)

No. of ways to go from B to C = 2 (IInd part)

$\therefore$ By Fundamental Principle of Counting, we can go from A to C via B in = 3 x 2 = 6 ways.

- To find the number of ways to attempt a job, divide the job into parts (parts for which we know that in how many ways each of them can be attempted).
- List the number of ways to attempt each of these parts, and then multiply all these to arrive at the answer.

- While listing the number of ways to attempt each part, list that part first which has some condition or has some speciality.
  For example:

(i) Let, we have to form 4-digit even numbers using the digits 1 to 9 without the repetition of digits. We know that even numbers have ONES place as a special position. Only the digits 2,4,6, and 8 can be chosen at ones place to make an even number. So, first we list the number of ways in which ones place can be filled, which is 4. Now all other places are ordinary places as any digit can be put there from the given digits. We can fill them in any order. As the number to be formed should not have repetition of digits so we will be left with only 8 digits after filling the ones place (*attention:* only one digit is used out of the four 2,4,6,8, and not all). Suppose we fill the TENS place now, which can be filled in 8 ways. After filling tens place, 7 digits will be left. So HUNDREDS place can be filled in 7 ways, which leaves 6 digits for Thousands place. So we can present our solution as follows:

Number of choices for ONES place = 4 ......(2,4,6,8)

Number of choices for TENS place = 8

Number of choices for HUNDREDS place = 7

Number of choices for THOUSANDS place = 6

$\therefore$ Total number of 4-digit numbers using digits 1 to 9 without repetition are $= 4 \times 8 \times 7 \times 6 = 1344$

(ii) If in the above example, we have to form the 4-digit even numbers in which repetition of digits is allowed , then after filling ones place each of remaining places can be filled in 9 ways. So the total number of 4-digit numbers using digits 1 to 9 are $= 4 \times 9 \times 9 \times 9 = 2916$

3   Permutations (Arrangements)

- The number of arrangements of n different things taken r at a time without repetition $= $ P (n , r) or we write it as $^n P_r$.

- We can easily find the formula of $^n P_r$ from Fundamental Principle of Counting, which is:

$$P\ (n , r) = {}^n P_r = \frac{n!}{(n-r)!} \quad , \qquad \text{where} \ \ 0 \le r \le n$$

---

*Asterisk (*) marked article (if any) is **not** in CBSE 2025-26 syllabus.*

- The number of arrangements of all n different things without repetition $= {}^{n}P_{n} = n!$
- The number of arrangements of n different objects at r places, when repetition is allowed $= n^{r}$.
- The number of arrangements of n different objects at n places, when repetition is allowed $= n^{n}$.
- The number of arrangements of n objects, where p_1 objects are of one kind, p_2 are of second kind, ..., p_k are of kth kind, and the rest, if any, are of different kind is

$$= \frac{n!}{p_1!\, p_2!\, p_3! \cdots p_k!}$$

4 Combinations (Selections)

- $C\,(n\,,\,r) = {}^{n}C_{r} = \dfrac{n!}{r!(n-r)!}$, where $\ 0 \le r \le n$

- The number of selections (Combinations) of n different things taken r at a time is $\ = C\,(n\,,\,r)$ or we write it as ${}^{n}C_{r}$

- ${}^{n}P_{r} = {}^{n}C_{r}\, r!$

- If $\ {}^{n}C_{a} = {}^{n}C_{b}$

  then $a = b$ or $a + b = n$

- ${}^{n}C_{r} + {}^{n}C_{r-1} = {}^{n+1}C_{r}$

- ${}^{n}C_{r} = {}^{n}C_{n-r}$

- ${}^{n}C_{0} = {}^{n}C_{n} = 1$

- ${}^{n}C_{1} = n$

Chapter-8　　　　Binomial Theorem

1　Binomial Theorem

For any positive integer n,

$$(a + b)^n = {}^nC_0\, a^n + {}^nC_1\, a^{n-1} b + {}^nC_2\, a^{n-2} b^2 + \ldots + {}^nC_{n-1}\, a\, b^{n-1}$$

$$+ {}^nC_n\, b^n$$

$$= \sum_{r=0}^{n} {}^nC_r\, a^{n-r}b^r$$

- The coefficients ${}^nC_r$ occuring in the binomial theorem are known as binomial coefficients.
- There are $(n+1)$ terms in the expansion of $(a+b)^n$, i.e., one more than the index n.
- The sum of the indices (powers) of a and b is n in every term of the binomial expansion of $(a+b)^n$

2　General Term

In the expansion of $(a + b)^n$,
- $(r + 1)^{\text{th}}$ term , $\qquad T_{r+1} = {}^nC_r\, a^{n-r}b^r$

3　Middle Term

In the expansion of $(a + b)^n$,
- if n is even , then total number of terms $n + 1$ is odd, and hence there will be one middle term, which is $\left(\dfrac{n+2}{2}\right)^{th}$ term .
- if n is odd , then total number of terms $n + 1$ is even, and hence there will be two middle terms , which are $\left(\dfrac{n+1}{2}\right)^{th}$ term and $\left(\dfrac{n+1}{2} + 1\right)^{th}$ term .

4　r^{th} term from the end

In the expansion of $(a + b)^n$,
- r^{th} term from the end is the $(n - r + 2)^{\text{th}}$ term from the beginning.

---

5 Other Results from Binomial Theorem

- $(a-b)^n = {}^nC_0 a^n + {}^nC_1 a^{n-1}(-b) + {}^nC_2 a^{n-2}(-b)^2 + {}^nC_3 a^{n-3}(-b)^3 +$

$$\ldots + {}^nC_n (-b)^n$$

$$= {}^nC_0 a^n - {}^nC_1 a^{n-1} b + {}^nC_2 a^{n-2} b^2 - {}^nC_3 a^{n-3} b^3 + \ldots + (-1)^n \, {}^nC_n b^n$$

- $(1+x)^n = {}^nC_0 + {}^nC_1 x + {}^nC_2 x^2 + {}^nC_3 x^3 \ldots + {}^nC_n x^n$

- By putting $x = 1$ in the expansion of $(1+x)^n$, we get the expansion of 2^n

$$2^n = {}^nC_0 + {}^nC_1 + {}^nC_2 + {}^nC_3 \ldots + {}^nC_n$$

- $(1-x)^n = {}^nC_0 - {}^nC_1 x + {}^nC_2 x^2 - {}^nC_3 x^3 \ldots + (-1)^n \, {}^nC_n x^n$

- By putting $x = 1$ in the expansion of $(1-x)^n$, we get

$$0 = {}^nC_0 - {}^nC_1 + {}^nC_2 - {}^nC_3 \ldots + (-1)^n \, {}^nC_n$$

Chapter-9   Sequences and Series

1 Sequence

An ordered collection of numbers, in which every number is identified by its position like 1st member, 2nd member, and so on, is called as sequence.

- A sequence can be regarded as a function whose domain is the set of natural numbers.
- The members of a sequence are called its terms and are usually, denoted as $a_1, a_2, a_3, \dots, a_n$, etc. Here, the subscripts denote the position of the term. i.e, the number at the nth position is n^{th} term and denoted as a_n .
- n^{th} term is also called its general term.

2 Series

If sequence is $a_1, a_2, a_3, \dots, a_n$,

then the expression $a_1 + a_2 + a_3 + \dots + a_n$ represents the **series** associated with the sequence.

3 Progression

Sequences, following specific patterns are called progressions.
For example, Arithmetic Progression, Geometric Progression, Harmonic Progression, etc.

4 Arithmetic Progression (A.P.)

If the difference between two successive terms of a sequence is constant , then the sequence is known as Arithmetic Progression.

- Constant difference between the successive terms is called the *common difference*.

4.1 Standard form of A.P.

- $a,\ a + d,\ a + 2d,\ a + 3d,\ \dots$
  where a = First Term and
           d = Common Difference

4.2   General Term

- n^{th} Term , $a_n = a + (n-1)\,d$

4.3   Sum of first n terms (S_n)

- $S_n = \dfrac{n}{2}\big[2a + (n-1)d\big]$

- $S_n = \dfrac{n}{2}(a + a_n)$

4.4   Some Properties of A.P.

- If a constant is added to each term of an A.P., the resulting sequence is also an A.P.
  i.e., if $a_1, a_2, a_3, \ldots, a_n$ are in A.P. ,

  then $a_1 + k, a_2 + k, a_3 + k, \ldots, a_n + k$ are also in A.P.

- If a constant is subtracted from each term of an A.P., the resulting sequence is also an A.P.
  i.e., if $a_1, a_2, a_3, \ldots, a_n$ are in A.P. ,

  then $a_1 - k, a_2 - k, a_3 - k, \ldots, a_n - k$ are also in A.P.

- If each term of an A.P. is multiplied by a constant, then the resulting sequence is also an A.P.
  i.e., if $a_1, a_2, a_3, \ldots, a_n$ are in A.P. ,

  then $a_1 k, a_2 k, a_3 k, \ldots, a_n k$ are also in A.P.

- If each term of an A.P. is divided by a non-zero constant, then the resulting sequence is also an A.P.
  i.e., if $a_1, a_2, a_3, \ldots, a_n$ are in A.P. , then

  $$\frac{a_1}{k}, \frac{a_2}{k}, \frac{a_3}{k}, \ldots, \frac{a_n}{k} \quad \text{are also in A.P.}$$

- If $S_n = S_m$,   then $S_{n+m} = 0$

- If there are n terms in an A.P. , then k^{th} term from the end is $(n-k+1)^{\text{th}}$ term from the beginning, and
  $$l_k = a + (n-k+1)\,d$$

  where l_k is k^{th} term from the end

---

*Asterisk (*) marked article (if any) is **not** in CBSE 2025-26 syllabus.*

5 Arithmetic Means (AMs)

If A_1, A_2, A_3, ..., A_n are n numbers between a and b

such that $a, A_1, A_2, A_3, \ldots, A_n, b$ is an A.P.,

then the numbers A_1, A_2, A_3, ..., A_n are known as *Arithmetic Means* (AMs) between a and b.

- The common difference of this A.P. will be $d = \dfrac{b-a}{n+1}$, where n is the number of AMs between a and b.

- The n AMs between a and b will be

$$A_1 = a + d = a + \frac{b-a}{n+1}$$

$$A_2 = a + 2d = a + 2\left(\frac{b-a}{n+1}\right)$$

$$A_3 = a + 3d = a + 3\left(\frac{b-a}{n+1}\right)$$

$$\vdots$$

$$A_n = a + nd = a + n\left(\frac{b-a}{n+1}\right)$$

6 AM between a and b

If A is a number between a and b such that a, A, b are in A.P., then A is known as Arithemetic Mean (AM) of a and b.

So, $$A = \frac{a+b}{2}$$

7 Geometric Progression (G.P.)

If the ratio of two successive terms of a sequence is constant, then the sequence is known as Geometric Progression.

- Constant ratio between the successive terms is called the *common ratio*.

7.1 Standard form of G.P.

- $a,\ ar,\ ar^2,\ ar^3, \ldots$
  where a = First Term and r = Common Ratio

*Asterisk (*) marked article (if any) is **not** in CBSE 2025-26 syllabus.*

7.2 General Term

n^{th} Term , $\quad a_n = a\, r^{n-1}$

7.3 Sum of first n terms (S_n)

$$S_n = \frac{a(r^n - 1)}{r - 1} = \frac{a(1 - r^n)}{1 - r}$$

7.4 Sum to infinity of G.P.

$$S_\infty = \frac{a}{1 - r} \qquad \text{if } |r| < 1$$

7.5 Some Properties of G.P.

- If each term of an G.P. is multiplied by a constant, then the resulting sequence is also an G.P.
  i.e., if $a_1, a_2, a_3, \ldots, a_n$ are in G.P. ,

  then $a_1 k, a_2 k, a_3 k, \ldots, a_n k$ are also in G.P.

- If each term of an G.P. is divided by a non-zero constant, then the resulting sequence is also an G.P.
  i.e., if $a_1, a_2, a_3, \ldots, a_n$ are in G.P. ,

  then $\dfrac{a_1}{k}, \dfrac{a_2}{k}, \dfrac{a_3}{k}, \ldots, \dfrac{a_n}{k}$ are also in G.P.

- If each term of an G.P. is raised to a constant power, then the resulting sequence is also an G.P.
  i.e., if $a_1, a_2, a_3, \ldots, a_n$ are in G.P. ,

  then $a_1{}^k, a_2{}^k, a_3{}^k, \ldots, a_n{}^k$ are also in G.P.

8 Geometric Means (GMs)

If $G_1, G_2, G_3, \ldots, G_n$ are n numbers between a and b such that $a, G_1, G_2, G_3, \ldots, G_n, b$ is a G.P. ,
then the numbers $G_1, G_2, G_3, \ldots, G_n$ are known as *Geometric Means* (AMs) between a and b .

- The common ratio of this A.P. will be $r = \left(\dfrac{b}{a}\right)^{\frac{1}{n+1}}$, where n is

  the number of GMs between a and b .

- The n GMs between a and b will be

$$G_1 = ar^2 = a\left(\frac{b}{a}\right)^{\frac{1}{n+1}}$$

$$G_2 = ar^2 = a\left(\frac{b}{a}\right)^{\frac{2}{n+1}}$$

$$G_3 = ar^3 = a\left(\frac{b}{a}\right)^{\frac{3}{n+1}}$$

$$\cdot$$

$$\cdot$$

$$\cdot$$

$$G_n = ar^n = a\left(\frac{b}{a}\right)^{\frac{n}{n+1}}$$

9   GM between a and b

If G is a number between a and b such that a, G, b are in G.P., then G is known as Geometric Mean (GM) of a and b.

So, $\qquad G = \pm\sqrt{ab}$

10   Relationship Between A.M. and G.M.

If A and G be A.M. and G.M. of two given positive real numbers a and b, respectively, then $A \geq G$

11   *Sum of first n terms of special series

- Sum of First n natural numbers:

$$\sum_{k=1}^{n} k = 1 + 2 + 3 + \ldots + n = \frac{n(n+1)}{2}$$

- Sum of Squares of First n natural numbers:

$$\sum_{k=1}^{n} k^2 = 1^2 + 2^2 + 3^2 + \ldots + n^2 = \frac{n(n+1)(2n+1)}{6}$$

- Sum of Cubes of First n natural numbers:

$$\sum_{k=1}^{n} k^3 = 1^3 + 2^3 + 3^3 + \ldots + n^3 = \left[\frac{n(n+1)}{2}\right]^2$$

Chapter-10   Straight Lines

1   Distance between two points

Distance between two points
$P(x_1, y_1)$ and $Q(x_1, y_1)$ is

$$PQ = \sqrt{(x_2 - x_1)^2 + (y_2 - y_1)^2}$$

2   Section Formula

2.1   Internal Division

If line segment joining $A(x_1, y_1)$ and $B(x_2, y_2)$ is divided by $P(x, y)$ in the ratio $m : n$ internally,

i.e., PA : PB $= m : n$ in the figure,

then

$$x = \frac{m\,x_2 + n\,x_1}{m + n}$$

$$y = \frac{m\,y_2 + n\,y_1}{m + n}$$

2.2   External Division

If line segment joining $A(x_1, y_1)$ and $B(x_2, y_2)$ is divided by $P(x, y)$ in the ratio $m : n$ externally,

i.e., PA : PB $= m : n$ in the figure, then

$$x = \frac{m\,x_2 - n\,x_1}{m - n}$$

$$y = \frac{m\,y_2 - n\,y_1}{m - n}$$

3   Mid - Point Formula

If P(x,y) is mid-point of line segment joining $A(x_1, y_1)$ and $B(x_2, y_2)$, then

$$x = \frac{x_1 + x_2}{2} \quad and \quad y = \frac{y_1 + y_2}{2}$$

4 Centroid of Triangle

If $A(x_1, y_1)$, $B(x_2, y_2)$ and $C(x_3, y_3)$ are vertices of a triangle, then coordinates of centroid $G(x, y)$ are :

$$x = \frac{x_1 + x_2 + x_3}{3} \quad \text{and} \quad y = \frac{y_1 + y_2 + y_3}{3}$$

5 *Incenter of Triangle

If $A(x_1, y_1)$, $B(x_2, y_2)$ and $C(x_3, y_3)$ are vertices of a triangle , then coordinates of its incentre $I(x, y)$ are

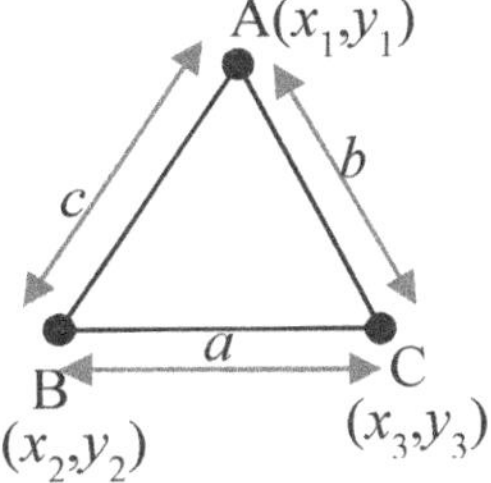

$$x = \frac{a\,x_1 + b\,x_2 + c\,x_3}{a + b + c}$$

$$y = \frac{a\,y_1 + b\,y_2 + c\,y_3}{a + b + c}$$

6 Area of Triangle

If $A(x_1, y_1)$, $B(x_2, y_2)$ and $C(x_3, y_3)$ are vertices of a triangle, then area of triangle is :

$$\Delta = \tfrac{1}{2}\,|\,x_1(y_2 - y_3) + x_2(y_3 - y_1) + x_3(y_1 - y_2)\,|$$

7 Slope of a Line *(m)*

(i) If θ = angle between the line and positive direction of $x - axis$,

then $m = tan\,\theta$

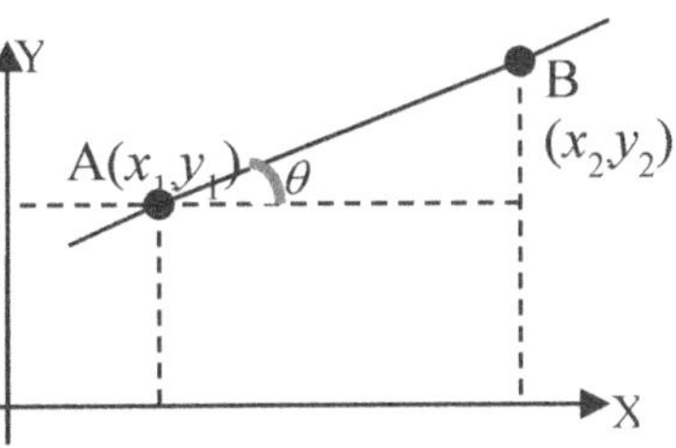

(ii) If $A(x_1, y_1)$ and $B(x_2, y_2)$ are 2 points on line ,

then $m = \dfrac{y_2 - y_1}{x_2 - x_1}$

8 Slope of x-*axis*

- $m = 0$
- Also slope of any line parallel to $x -$ axis $= 0$

9 Slope of y - *axis*

- m = not defined
- Also slope of any line parallel to y – axis = not defined

10 Conditions for collinearity

We can show that the points $A(x_1, y_1)$, $B(x_2, y_2)$ and $C(x_3, y_3)$ are collinear by any of the following ways:

(i) By **Distance formula :**

$$AB + BC = AC \quad \text{or} \quad AB + AC = BC \quad \text{or} \quad BC + AC = AB$$

(ii) By **Area of Triangle :**

area of $\Delta = 0$

$$x_1(y_2 - y_3) + x_2(y_3 - y_1) + x_3(y_1 - y_2) = 0$$

(iii) By **Slope of line :**

Slope of AB $=$ Slope of BC

11 Condition for parallel and perpendicular lines

If m_1 and m_2 are slopes of 2 lines , then

(i) for **Parallel Lines :** $\qquad m_1 = m_2$

(ii) for Perpendicular Lines : $\qquad m_1 . m_2 = -1$

12 Acute Angle (θ) between two lines

If θ is acute angle between two lines, and m_1 and m_2 are their slopes, then

$$tan\theta = \left| \frac{m_2 - m_1}{1 + m_1 m_2} \right|$$

- If $tan\,\theta$ is $+$ve , then θ is the acute angle between the lines.
- If $tan\,\theta$ is $-$ve , then θ is the obtuse angle between the lines.

13 Equations of straight lines
13.1 Equations of lines parallel to x and y axes

(i) Equation of line parallel to x – *axis* through a point (a, b) is
$y = b$

(ii) Equation of line parallel to y – *axis* through a point (a, b) is
$x = a$

13.2 Slope – Point Form

If m = slope of line and (x_1, y_1) is a point on line ,

then equation of line is:
$$\frac{y - y_1}{x - x_1} = m$$

13.3 Two Point Form

If (x_1, y_1) and (x_2, y_2) are 2 points on line ,

then equation of line is:
$$\frac{y - y_1}{x - x_1} = \frac{y_2 - y_1}{x_2 - x_1}$$

13.4 Intercept Form

If a = x – intercept
and b = y – intercept ,

then equation of line is:

$$\frac{x}{a} + \frac{y}{b} = 1$$

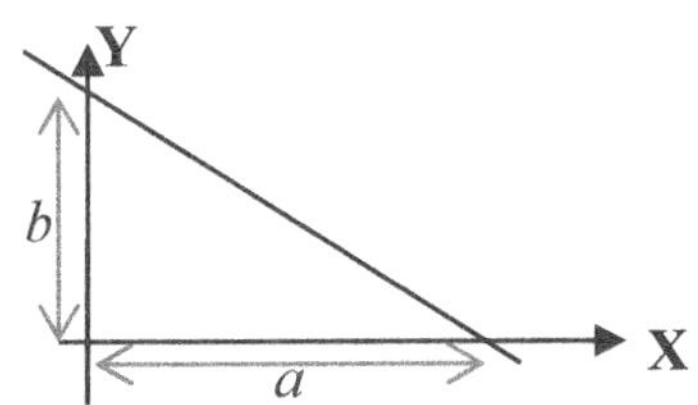

13.5 Slope – intercept Form

(i) **Slope and y – intercept Form:**

If m = slope of line and b = y – intercept ,

then equation of line is: $y = m x + b$

(ii) **Slope and x – intercept Form:**

If m = slope of line and a = x – intercept ,

then equation of line is: $y = m (x - a)$

13.6 *Normal Form

If ω = angle made by normal from
origin with + ve direction of x–axis

and p = length of perpendicular
(normal) from origin ,

then equation of line is:

$x \cos \omega + y \sin \omega = p$

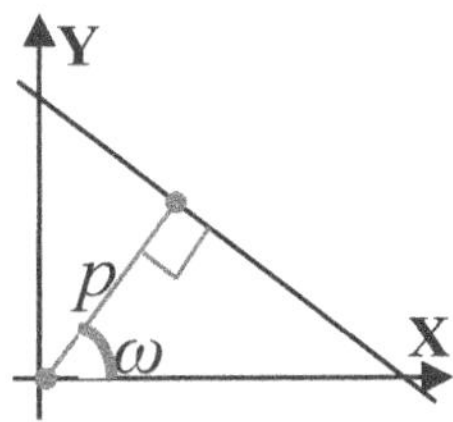

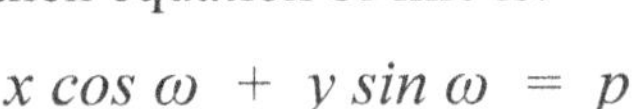

*Asterisk (*) marked article (if any) is **not** in CBSE 2025-26 syllabus.*

13.7 *Symmetric Form

If (x_1, y_1) is a point on line , and

θ = angle between the line and positive $x-axis$,

then equation of line is: $\dfrac{x - x_1}{\cos \theta} = \dfrac{y - y_1}{\sin \theta} = r$ (say)

- r will be the distance between (x, y) and (x_1, y_1)

14 General Form

$A\,x + B\,y + C = 0$

- Slope : $m = -\dfrac{A}{B}$
- x – intercept : $a = -\dfrac{C}{A}$
- y – intercept : $b = -\dfrac{C}{B}$

15 Distance of a Point from a Line

$$D = \frac{|A\,x_1 + B\,y_1 + C|}{\sqrt{A^2 + B^2}}$$

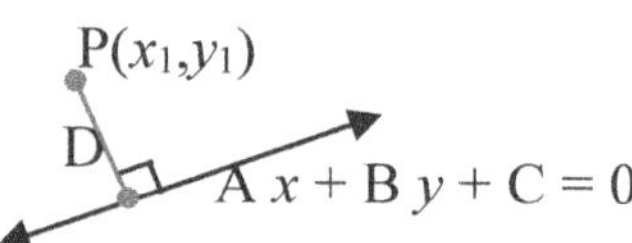

16 Distance between Two Parallel Line

$$D = \frac{|C_1 - C_2|}{\sqrt{A^2 + B^2}}$$

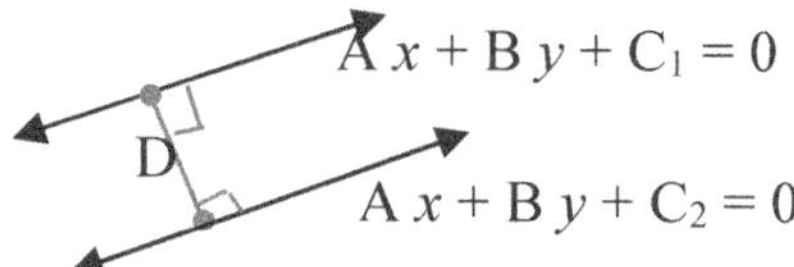

Chapter-11   Conic Sections

1   Circle

A circle is a set (or locus) of all points in a plane that are equidistant from a fixed point in the plane.

- The fixed point is called the *centre* of the circle, and the distance from the centre to a point on the circle is called the *radius* of the circle.

1.1   Standard Equation

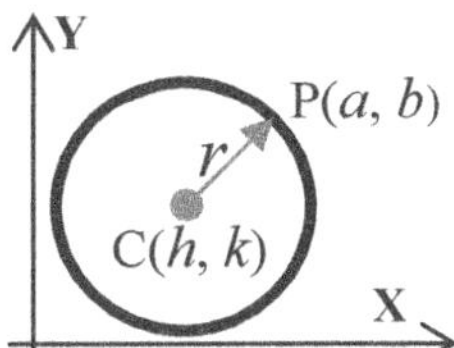

- $(x - h)^2 + (y - k)^2 = r^2$
  where, centre $= (h, k)$
  and   radius $= r$

1.2   General Equation

- $x^2 + y^2 + 2gx + 2fy + c = 0$
  where, centre $= (-g, -f)$ and radius $= \sqrt{g^2 + f^2 - c}$

1.3   Point lying inside, outside or on the circle

Let Centre be C(h, k), radius $= r$ and a given point be P(a, b)

Find distance $CP = \sqrt{(a - h)^2 + (b - k)^2}$

- If the distance $CP < r$, then point P lies inside the circle.
- If the distance $CP > r$, then point P lies outside the circle.
- If the distance $CP = r$, then point P lies on the circle.

2 Parabola

A parabola is a set (or locus) of all points in a plane that are equidistant from a fixed line and a fixed point (not on the line) in the plane.

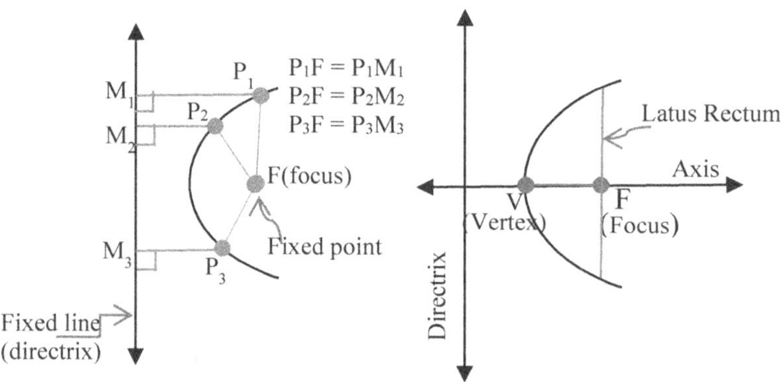

- The fixed line is called the *directrix* of the parabola, and the fixed point, F is called the *focus*.
- A line through the focus and perpendicular to the directrix is called the *axis* of the parabola.
- The point of intersection of parabola with the axis is called the *vertex* of the parabola.
- The chord passing through the focus and perpendicular to the axis is called the *latus rectum*.

2.1 Standard Equations

If the vertex of the parabola is at the origin, and the axis of symmetry is along the x-axis or y-axis , then the equation of the parabola is the simplest, and there are 4 such simplest equations, which are known as *standard equations*.

(i) $y^2 = 4ax$, $a > 0$
(ii) $y^2 = -4ax$, $a > 0$
(iii) $x^2 = 4ay$, $a > 0$
(iv) $x^2 = -4ay$, $a > 0$

Characteristics and curves of these equations are as follows:

2.1.1 Equation: $y^2 = 4ax$, $a > 0$

Vertex (V)	(0 , 0)
Axis	X-axis or $y=0$ (right of Y-axis)
Focus (F)	(a , 0)
Equation of Directrix	$x = -a$
Length of Latus Rectum	$4a$

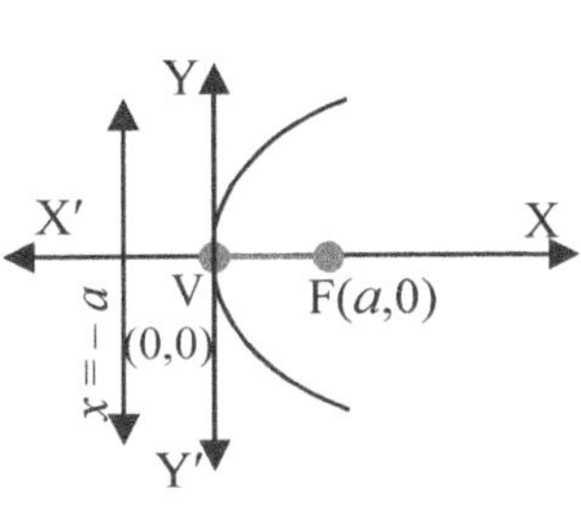

2.1.2 Equation: $y^2 = -4ax$, $a > 0$

Vertex	(0 , 0)
Axis	X-axis or $y = 0$ (left of Y-axis)
Focus	($-a$, 0)
Equation of Directrix	$x = a$
Length of Latus Rectum	$4a$

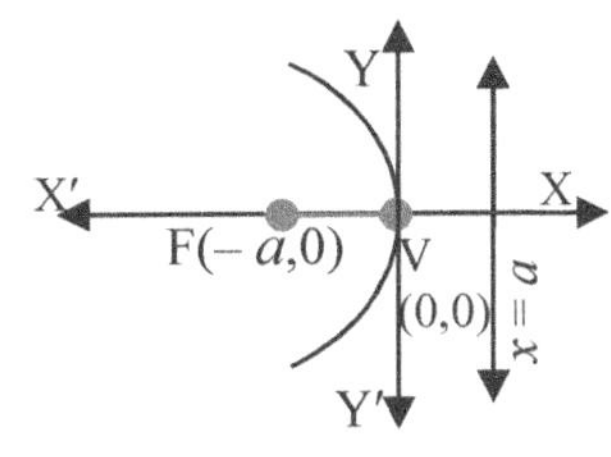

2.1.3 Equation: $x^2 = 4ay$, $a > 0$

Vertex	(0 , 0)
Axis	Y-axis or $x = 0$ (above X-axis)
Focus	(0 , a)
Equation of Directrix	$y = -a$
Length of Latus Rectum	$4a$

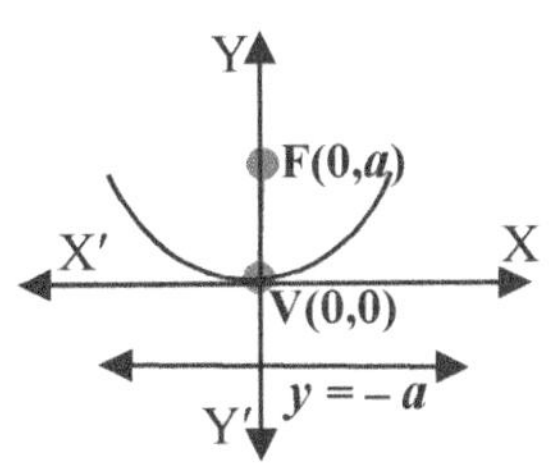

---

*Asterisk (*) marked article (if any) is **not** in CBSE 2025-26 syllabus.*

2.1.4 Equation: $\quad x^2 = -4ay$, $a > 0$

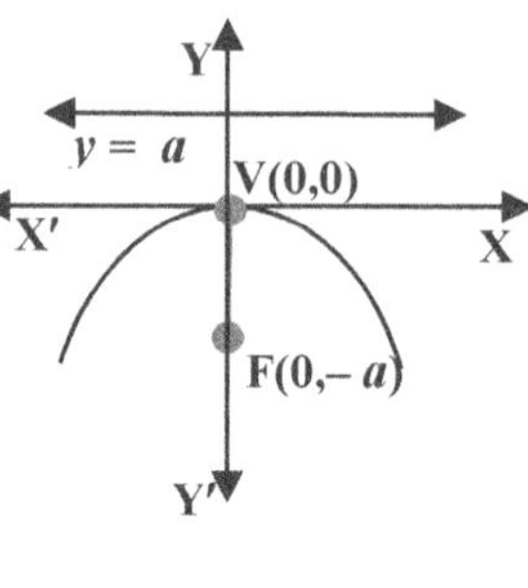

Vertex	$(0,0)$
Axis	Y-axis or $x = 0$ (below X-axis)
Focus	$(0,-a)$
Equation of Directrix	$y = a$
Length of Latus Rectum	$4a$

3 Ellipse

An ellipse is a set of all points in a plane, the sum of whose distances from two fixed points in the plane is a constant.

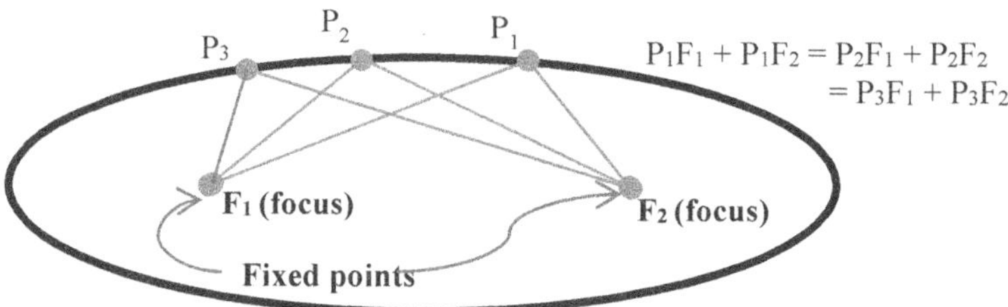

- The two fixed points are called the *foci* (plural of '*focus*') of the ellipse.
- The mid-point of the line segment joining the foci is called the *centre* of the ellipse.
- The line segment through the foci of the ellipse with end points on the ellipse is called the *major axis*, and the line segment through the centre and perpendicular to the major axis with end points on the ellipse is called the *minor axis*.

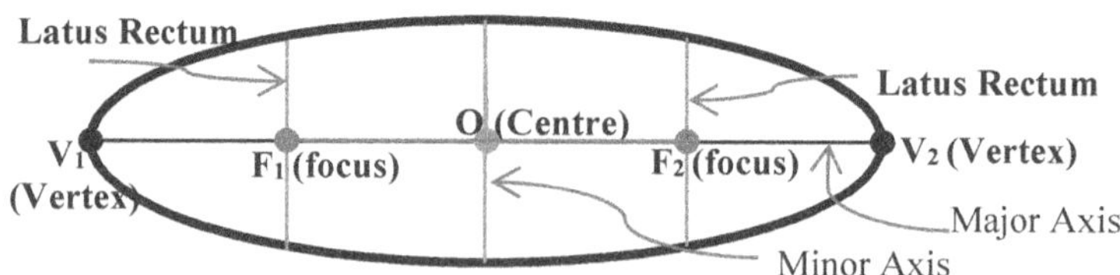

---

*Asterisk (*) marked article (if any) is **not** in CBSE 2025-26 syllabus.*

- The end points of the major axis are called the *vertices* of the ellipse.
- The chord passing through a focus and perpendicular to the major axis is called the *latus rectum*. There are two latus rectums.
- The ratio of the distances of a focus and a vertex from the centre is called the *eccentricity* of the ellipse. It denoted by e .

$$\text{So, } e = \frac{c}{a}$$

Where, c = distance of focus from the centre, and a = distance of vertex from the centre

3.1 Standard Equations

If the centre of the ellipse is at the origin, and the foci lie on the x-axis or y-axis , then the equation of the ellipse is the simplest, and there are 2 such simplest equations, which are known as *standard equations*.

(i) $\dfrac{x^2}{a^2} + \dfrac{y^2}{b^2} = 1$, $a > 0$, $b > 0$, $a > b$

(ii) $\dfrac{y^2}{a^2} + \dfrac{x^2}{b^2} = 1$, $a > 0$, $b > 0$, $a > b$

Characteristics and curves of these equations are as follows:

3.1.1 Equation: $\dfrac{x^2}{a^2} + \dfrac{y^2}{b^2} = 1$, $a > 0$, $b > 0$, $a > b$

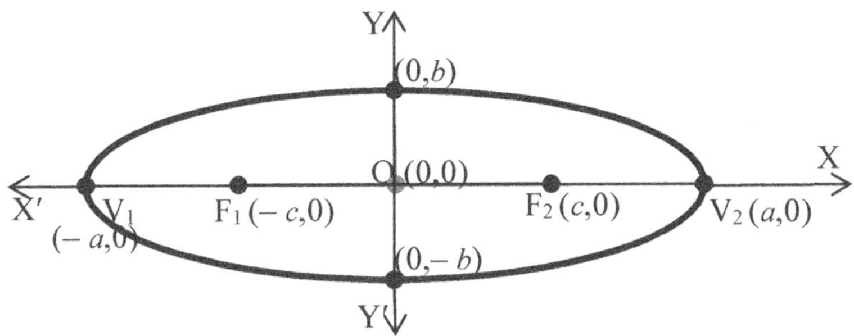

Centre	$(0,0)$
Vertices (Ends of Major Axis)	$(\pm a, 0)$
Ends of Minor Axis	$(0, \pm b)$
Major axis	Along X-axis (Eqn. $y = 0$)
Minor axis	Along Y-axis (Eqn. $x = 0$)
Foci	$(\pm c, 0)$ or $(\pm ae, 0)$
Length of Major axis	$2a$
Length of Minor axis	$2b$
Length of Latus Rectum	$\dfrac{2b^2}{a}$
Important Relation	(i) $c^2 = a^2 - b^2$ (ii) $b^2 = a^2(1 - e^2)$ (iii) $c = ae$ (iv) $0 < c < a$ (v) $0 < e < 1$

3.1.2 Equation: $\dfrac{y^2}{a^2} + \dfrac{x^2}{b^2} = 1,\ a > 0,\ b > 0,\ a > b$

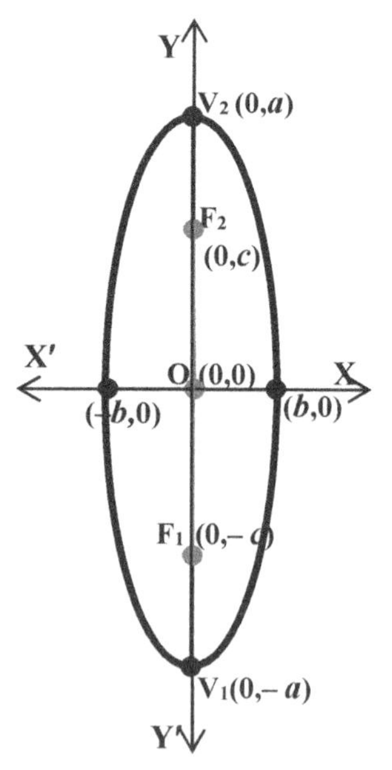

Centre	$(0,0)$
Vertices (Ends of Major Axis)	$(0, \pm a)$
Ends of Minor Axis	$(\pm b, 0)$
Major axis	Along Y-axis (Eqn. $x = 0$)
Minor axis	Along X-axis (Eqn. $y = 0$)
Foci	$(0, \pm c)$ or $(0, \pm ae)$
Length of Major axis	$2a$
Length of Minor axis	$2b$
Length of Latus Rectum	$\dfrac{2b^2}{a}$
Important Relations	(i) $c^2 = a^2 - b^2$ (ii) $b^2 = a^2(1 - e^2)$ (iii) $c = ae$ (iv) $0 < c < a$ (v) $0 < e < 1$

4 Hyperbola

A hyperbola is a set of all points in a plane, the difference of whose distances from two fixed points in the plane is a constant.

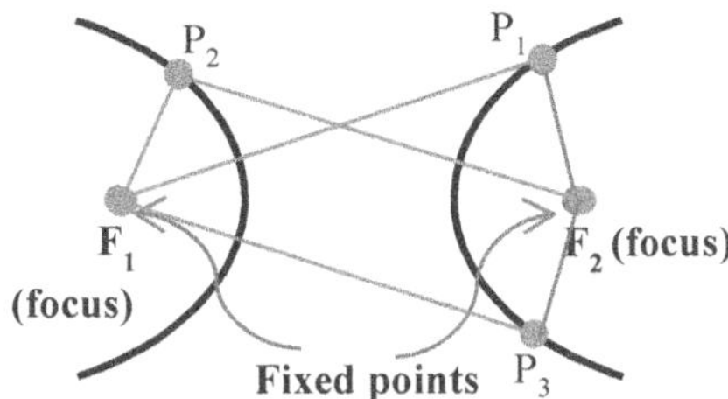

$$P_1F_1 - P_1F_2 = P_2F_2 - P_2F_1 = P_3F_1 - P_3F_2$$

- The two fixed points are called the *foci* of the hyperbola.
- The mid-point of the line segment joining the foci is called the *centre* of the hyperbola.
- The line segment through the foci of the hyperbola with end points on the hyperbola is called the *transverse axis*, and the line segment through the centre and perpendicular to the transverse axis is called the *conjugate axis*.

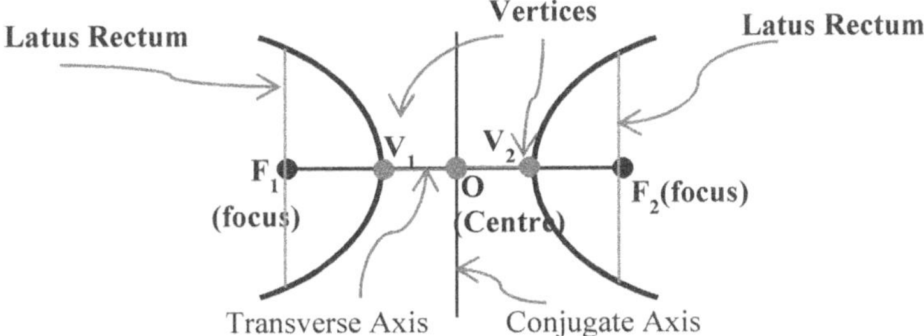

- The end points of the transverse axis are called the *vertices* of the hyperbola.
- The chord passing through a focus and perpendicular to the transverse axis is called the *latus rectum*. There are two latus rectums.
- The ratio of the distances of a focus and a vertex from the centre is called the *eccentricity* of the hyperbola. It denoted by e .

$$\text{So, } e = \frac{c}{a}$$

Where, c = distance of focus from the centre, and a = distance of vertex from the centre

---

4.1   Standard Equations

If the centre of the hyperbola is at the origin, and the foci lie on the x-axis or y-axis , then the equation of the hyperbola is the simplest, and there are 2 such simplest equations, which are known *standard equations*.

(i) $\dfrac{x^2}{a^2} - \dfrac{y^2}{b^2} = 1,\ \ a > 0 , b > 0$

(ii) $\dfrac{y^2}{a^2} - \dfrac{x^2}{b^2} = 1,\ \ a > 0 , b > 0$

Characteristics and curves of these equations are as follows:

4.1.1   Equation: $\dfrac{x^2}{a^2} - \dfrac{y^2}{b^2} = 1,$ $a > 0 , b > 0$

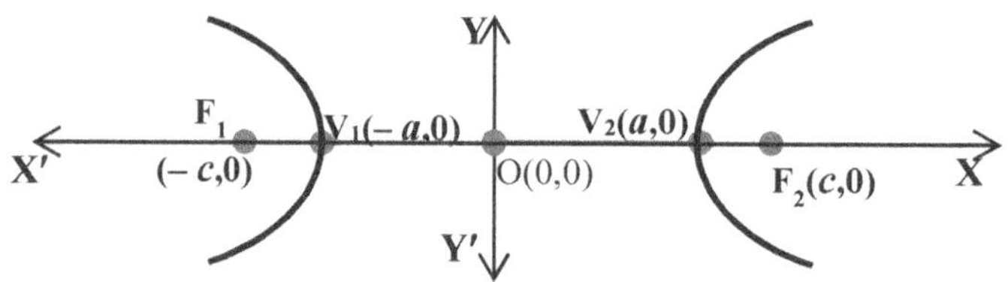

Centre	$(0 , 0)$
Vertices	$(\pm a , 0)$
Transverse axis	Along X-axis (Eqn. $y = 0$)
Conjugate axis	Along Y-axis (Eqn. $x = 0$)
Foci	$(\pm c , 0)$ or $(\pm ae , 0)$
Length of Transverse axis	$2a$
Length of Conjugate axis	$2b$
Length of Latus Rectum	$\dfrac{2b^2}{a}$
Important Relations	(i) $c^2 = a^2 + b^2$ (ii) $b^2 = a^2(e^2 - 1)$ (iii) $c = ae$ (iv) $c > a$ (v) $e > 1$

4.1.2 Equation: $\dfrac{y^2}{a^2} - \dfrac{x^2}{b^2} = 1,\ a > 0,\ b > 0$

Centre	$(\,0\,,\,0\,)$
Vertices	$(\,0\,,\,\pm a\,)$
Transverse axis	Along Y-axis (Eqn. $x = 0$)
Conjugate axis	Along X-axis (Eqn. $y = 0$)
Foci	$(\,0\,,\,\pm c\,)$ or $(\,0\,,\,\pm ae\,)$
Length of Transverse axis	$2a$
Length of Conjugate axis	$2b$
Length of Latus Rectum	$\dfrac{2b^2}{a}$
Important Relations	(i) $c^2 = a^2 + b^2$ (ii) $b^2 = a^2(e^2 - 1)$ (iii) $c = ae$ (iv) $c > a$ (v) $e > 1$

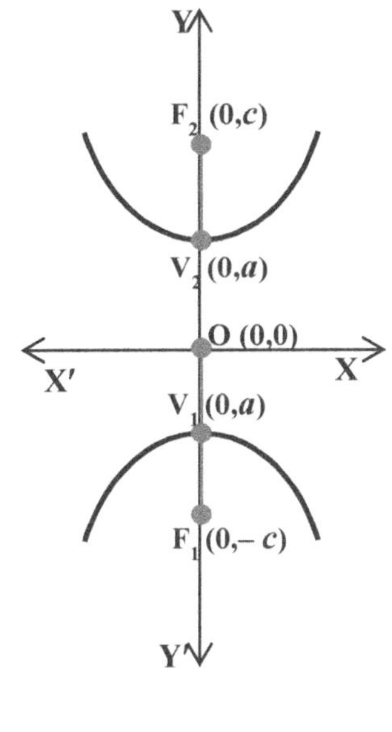

Chapter-12   Three-Dimensional Geometry

1   Basic Concepts

We can locate any point in space using three mutually perpendicular lines, which are known as Coordinate axes. These coordinate axes are X-axis, Y-axis and Z-axis.

- Their point of intersection is known as origin O whose coordinates are marked as (0,0,0).
- These three axes determine three mutually perpendicular planes called Coordinate planes.

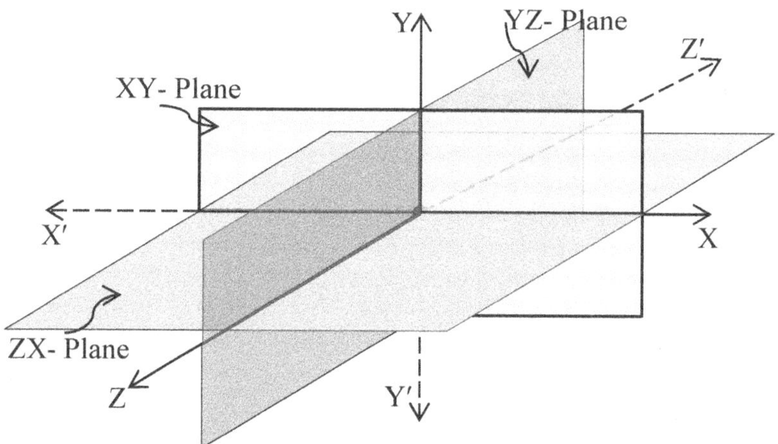

- These planes are:
  (i) XY-plane or XOY which contains X and Y axes
  (ii) YZ plane or YOZ which contains Y and Z axes, and
  (iii)ZX-plane ZOX which contains Z and X axes.
- We can take the plane of paper as XOY plane, and consider it to be horizontal.
- The X-axis towards right of origin O is positive X-axis and is denoted as OX.

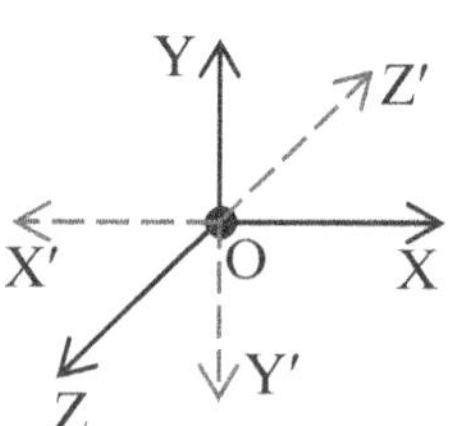

The X-axis towards left of O is negative X-axis and is denoted as OX'.

The complete X-axis can be denoted as X'OX.

- The Y-axis above the origin O (towards top of paper) is positive Y-axis and is denoted as OY.

    The Y-axis below the origin O (towards bottom of paper) is negative Y-axis and is denoted as OY'.

    The complete Y-axis can be denoted as Y'OY.

- Z-axis is perpendicular to XOY plane, and if XOY plane is horizontal , then Z-axis will be vertical through O.

- The Z-axis in the vertically upward direction from XOY plane (perpendicularly outwards from the plane of paper) is positive Z-axis and is denoted as OZ

    The Z-axis in the vertically downward direction from XOY plane (perpendicularly inwards to the plane of paper) is negative Z-axis and is denoted as OZ'.

    The complete Z-axis can be denoted as Z'OZ.

- The planes divide the space into eight parts known as octants. These octants are could be named as XOYZ, X'OYZ, X'OY'Z, XOY'Z, XOYZ', X'OYZ', X'OY'Z' and XOY'Z' , and denoted by I, II, III, IV, V, VI, VII and VIII , respectively.

- If P is a point in the space, then

    (i)   its perpendicular distance from the YZ plane represents its x-coordinate.

    (ii) its perpendicular distance from the ZX plane represents its y-coordinate.

    (iii) its perpendicular distance from the XY plane represents its z-coordinate.

    (iv) the coordinates of P are written as (x, y, z)

- Coordinates of a point lying

    (i)   on X-axis are in the form ($x, 0, 0$).

    (ii) on Y-axis are in the form ($0, y, 0$).

    (iii) on Z-axis are in the form ($0, 0, z$).

- Coordinates of a point lying

    (i)   on XY-plane are in the form ($x, y, 0$).

    (ii) on YZ plane are in the form ($0, y, z$).

    (iii) on ZX-plane are in the form ($x, 0, z$).

- The coordinates of the foot of perpendicular of point P(a, b, c)

    (i)   on XY-plane are ($a, b, 0$).

    (ii) on YZ plane are ($0, b, c$).

    (iii) on ZX-plane are ($a, 0, c$).

- The signs of x, y and z coordinates in eight octants are as shown in the table:

Coordinates \ Quadrants	I	II	III	IV	V	VI	VII	VIII
x	+	−	−	+	+	−	−	+
y	+	+	−	−	+	+	−	−
z	+	+	+	+	−	−	−	−

2 Distance between two points

Distance between two points $P(x_1, y_1, z_1)$ and $Q(x_1, y_1, z_2)$ is

$$PQ = \sqrt{(x_2 - x_1)^2 + (y_2 - y_1)^2 + (z_2 - z_1)^2}$$

3 *Section Formula

3.1 *Internal Division

If line segment joining $A(x_1, y_1, z_1)$ and $B(x_2, y_2, z_2)$ is divided by $P(x, y, z)$ in the ratio $m : n$ internally,

i.e., PA : PB $= m : n$ in the figure,

then

$$x = \frac{m\, x_2 + n\, x_1}{m + n}$$

$$y = \frac{m\, y_2 + n\, y_1}{m + n}$$

$$z = \frac{m\, z_2 + n\, z_1}{m + n}$$

3.2 *External Division

If line segment joining $A(x_1, y_1, z_1)$ and $B(x_2, y_2, z_2)$ is divided by $P(x, y, z)$ in the ratio $m : n$ externally, i.e., PA : PB $= m : n$ in the figure, then

$$x = \frac{m\,x_2 - n\,x_1}{m - n}$$

$$y = \frac{m\,y_2 - n\,y_1}{m - n}$$

$$z = \frac{m\,z_2 - n\,z_1}{m - n}$$

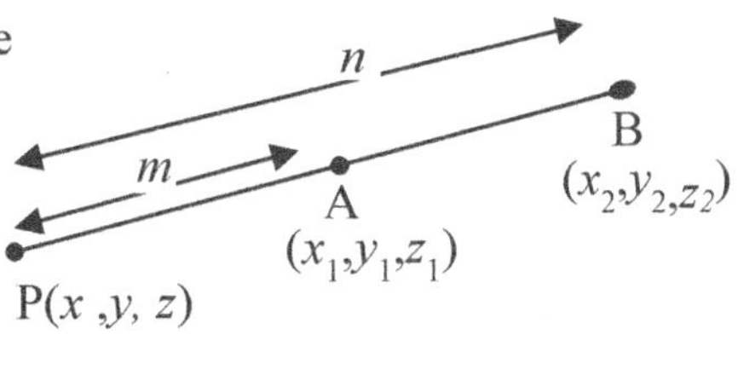

4   *Mid - Point Formula

If $P(x, y, z)$ is mid-point of line segment joining $A(x_1, y_1, z_1)$ and $B(x_2, y_2, z_2)$, then

$$x = \frac{x_1 + x_2}{2}$$

$$y = \frac{y_1 + y_2}{2}$$

$$z = \frac{z_1 + z_2}{2}$$

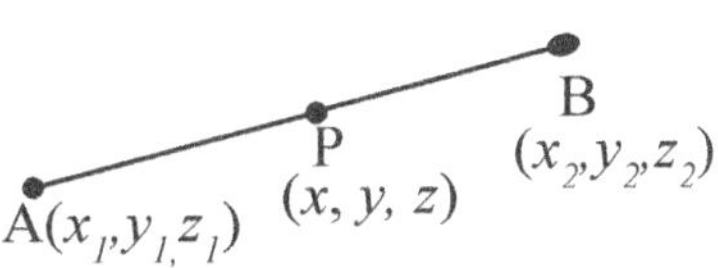

5   *Centroid of Triangle

If $A(x_1, y_1, z_1)$, $B(x_2, y_2, z_2)$ and $C(x_3, y_3, z_3)$ are vertices of a triangle , then coordinates of centroid $G(x, y, z)$ are :

$$x = \frac{x_1 + x_2 + x_3}{3}, \qquad y = \frac{y_1 + y_2 + y_3}{3}, \qquad z = \frac{z_1 + z_2 + z_3}{3}$$

6   *Incenter of Triangle

If A (x_1, y_1, z_1) , B (x_2, y_2, z_2) and C (x_3, y_3, z_3) are vertices of a triangle , then coordinates of incenter I(x, y, z) are :

$$x = \frac{a\,x_1 + b\,x_2 + c\,x_3}{a+b+c}$$

$$y = \frac{a\,y_1 + b\,y_2 + c\,y_3}{a + b + c}$$

$$z = \frac{a\,z_1 + b\,z_2 + c\,z_3}{a + b + c}$$

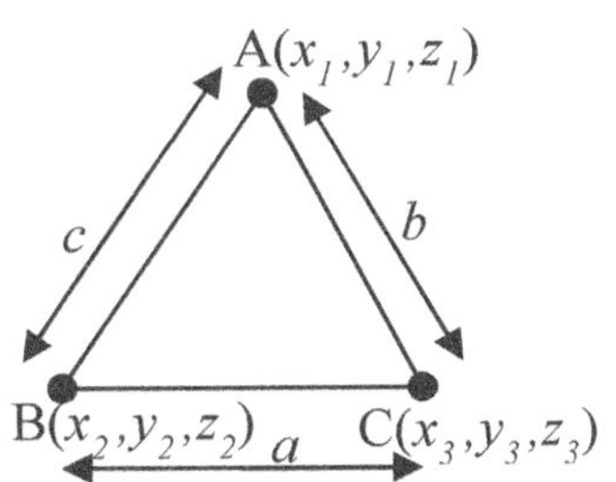

---

*Asterisk (*) marked article (if any) is **not** in CBSE 2025-26 syllabus.*

Chapter-13 Limits

1 Concept of Limit and its Explanation

Suppose we want to find the value of a function $f(x)$ when the value of x tends to become very close to a. We write this situation as $\lim_{x \to a} f(x)$, and read it as Limit of $f(x)$ as x approaches to a.

- When we say that x is very close to a (or x approaches to a), it may have value which is slightly less than a or slightly greater than a. It means that x may be approaching to a from left of a on the number line or from right of a.

  Accordingly, there could be two types of limits:

  (i) **Left Hand Limit:** When x is approaching to a from left, we call the value of function as Left Hand Limit of the function at $x = a$.

  We write it as $\lim_{x \to a^-} f(x)$

  (ii) **Right Hand Limit:** When x is approaching to a from right, we call the value of function as Right Hand Limit of the function at $x = a$.

  We write it as $\lim_{x \to a^+} f(x)$

- In general, if Left Hand Limit and Right Hand Limit of a function $f(x)$ is same at $x = a$, then we say that the limit of function exists at $x = a$.

  If $\lim_{x \to a^-} f(x) = l$ and $\lim_{x \to a^+} f(x) = l$,

  then $\lim_{x \to a} f(x)$ *exists* and $\lim_{x \to a} f(x) = l.$

2 Algebra of Limits

If the limit of two functions f and g exist at $x = a$, then limit of their sum, difference, and product also exist at $x = a$ and are, respectively equal to sum, difference, and product of their limits. Limit of their quotient also exists provided the quotient does not become zero at $x = a$.

i.e., if $\lim_{x \to a} f(x)$ and $\lim_{x \to a} g(x)$ both exist, then

(i) $\lim_{x \to a} [\, f(x) + g(x) \,] = \lim_{x \to a} f(x) + \lim_{x \to a} g(x).$

(ii) $\lim_{x \to a} [\, f(x) - g(x) \,] = \lim_{x \to a} f(x) - \lim_{x \to a} g(x).$

*Asterisk (*) marked article (if any) is **not** in CBSE 2025-26 syllabus.*

(iii) $\lim\limits_{x \to a} [\, f(x) . g(x)\,] = \lim\limits_{x \to a} f(x) . \lim\limits_{x \to a} g(x)$.

Also $\lim\limits_{x \to a} [\, \lambda . f(x)\,] = \lambda . \lim\limits_{x \to a} f(x)$, where λ is a real number

(iv) $\lim\limits_{x \to a} \dfrac{f(x)}{g(x)} = \dfrac{\lim\limits_{x \to a} f(x)}{\lim\limits_{x \to a} g(x)}$ provided $\lim\limits_{x \to a} g(x) \neq 0$

3   Limit of Polynomial Function

A function f is said to be a polynomial function if $f(x)$ is zero function or if $f(x) = a_0 + a_1 x + a_2 x^2 + \ldots + a_n x^n$, where $a_0, a_1, a_2, \ldots, a_n$ are real numbers such that $a_n \neq 0$ for some natural number n.

For a polynomial function $f(x)$: $\lim\limits_{x \to a} f(x) = f(a)$

At every real number, Left Hand Limit and Right Hand Limit of a polynomial function are always same.

Therefore, Limit of a polynomial function exists at every real number, and it is equal to the value of the function exactly at that number.

3.1   Procedure to find limit of polynomial function

We can calculate the limit of a polynomial function $f(x)$ by just putting the value of x in the function.

It means that $\lim\limits_{x \to a} f(x) = f(a)$

4   Limit of Rational Function

A function f is said to be a rational function if $f(x) = \dfrac{g(x)}{h(x)}$, where $g(x)$ and $h(x)$ are polynomial functions such that $h(x) \neq 0$

For a rational function $f(x) = \dfrac{g(x)}{h(x)}$: $\lim\limits_{x \to a} f(x) = \dfrac{\lim\limits_{x \to a} g(x)}{\lim\limits_{x \to a} h(x)}$

- if $h(a) \neq 0$, then $\lim\limits_{x \to a} f(x) = \dfrac{g(a)}{h(a)}$
- if $h(a) = 0$ but $g(a) \neq 0$, then $\lim\limits_{x \to a} f(x)$ is not defined.

- if $h(a) = 0$ and $g(a) = 0$, then we will be able to factorize $h(x)$ & $g(x)$ having one or more times the factor $(x - a)$ in them, and write $h(x) = (x - a)^k h_1(x)$ and $g(x) = (x - a)^l g_1(x)$.

So, we will write $\displaystyle \lim_{x \to a} f(x) = \frac{\lim_{x \to a}(x-a)^l \, g_1(x)}{\lim_{x \to a}(x-a)^k \, h_1(x)}$.

- If $l > k$, then after cancelling common factors in numerator and denominator, $(x - a)$ will still be left in the numerator, and hence when we put $x = a$ we get
$$\lim_{x \to a} f(x) = 0$$

- If $l < k$, then after cancelling common factors in numerator and denominator, $(x - a)$ will still be left in the denominator, and hence when we put $x = a$, we get
$$\lim_{x \to a} f(x) = \text{not defined.}$$

4.1 Procedure to find limit of rational function

- We can calculate the limit of a rational function by just putting the value of x in the function if denominator does not become 0.
- If denominator becomes 0 by putting the value of x, then first factorize both numerator and denominator, and cancel out all common factors. Now put the value of x in it. If denominator still becomes 0 , then limit of the function is not defined at that value of x. If denominator does not become 0 then the value obtained is the limit of function at that value of x.

5 Sandwich Theorem

Let f, g and h be real functions such that $f(x) \le g(x) \le h(x)$ for all x in their common domain.

For some real number a,

if $\displaystyle \lim_{x \to a} f(x) = 1 = \lim_{x \to a} h(x)$, then

$$\lim_{x \to a} g(x) = l.$$

6   Important Limits

(i) $\lim\limits_{x\to a} \dfrac{x^n - a^n}{x-a} = n\,a^{\,n-1}$

    (for all rational number n and a being any positive number)

    Also $\lim\limits_{x\to a} \dfrac{x-a}{x^n - a^n} = \dfrac{1}{n\,a^{n-1}}$

(ii) $\lim\limits_{x\to 0} \dfrac{sinx}{x} = 1$ (where angle x is in radians)

    Also $\lim\limits_{x\to 0} \dfrac{x}{sinx} = 1$

(iii) $\lim\limits_{x\to 0} \dfrac{e^x - 1}{x} = 1$

    Also $\lim\limits_{x\to 0} \dfrac{x}{e^x - 1} = 1$

(iv) $\lim\limits_{x\to 0} \dfrac{a^x - 1}{x} = log_e\, a$

    Also $\lim\limits_{x\to 0} \dfrac{x}{a^x - 1} = \dfrac{1}{log_e\, a}$

(v) $\lim\limits_{x\to 0} \dfrac{log_e|1+x|}{x} = 1$

    Also $\lim\limits_{x\to 0} \dfrac{x}{log_e|1+x|} = 1$

(vi) $\lim\limits_{x\to 0} \dfrac{log_a|1+x|}{x} = \dfrac{1}{log_e\, a}$

    Also $\lim\limits_{x\to 0} \dfrac{x}{log_a|1+x|} = log_e\, a$

Chapter-14   Derivatives

1   Concept of Derivatives and its Explanation

Let f be a real function of x. We can write it as $y = f(x)$. If there is a change in x, then there will be a change in y. We write change in x as Δx and change in y as Δy.

When the value of x changes from x to $x + \Delta x$, the change in y per unit change in x will be $\dfrac{\Delta y}{\Delta x}$.

Now, if we want to find the rate at which y is changing with respect to x at a particular value of x (say, at $x = a$), then the change (Δx) in the value of x from a should be so small that change occurring in y can be considered just at $x = a$, i.e., we should find $\dfrac{\Delta y}{\Delta x}$ when Δx approaches to 0.

We represent this situation as $\lim\limits_{\Delta x \to 0} \dfrac{\Delta y}{\Delta x}$ when $x = a$.

It is called the *derivative* of y with respect to x at $x = a$

- $\dfrac{dy}{dx}\bigg|_{x=a}$ represents *derivative* of y with respect to x at $x = a$
- In general, *derivative* of y with respect to x, at any value of x, is represented as $\dfrac{dy}{dx}$

$$\therefore \quad \frac{dy}{dx} = \lim_{\Delta x \to 0} \frac{\Delta y}{\Delta x}.$$

If we do not write the function $f(x)$ as y, then the modifications in the whole concept explained above will be as follows:

Here for convenience, we can write Δx as h.

If the value of x changes from a to $a + h$ such that h approaches to 0, then the value of $f(x)$ changes from $f(a)$ to $f(a + h)$.

So, change in the function f is $= f(a + h) - f(a)$
and at $x = a$, the change in f per unit change in x is given by

$$\lim_{h \to 0} \frac{f(a + h) - f(a)}{h}$$

This is the derivative of $f(x)$ at $x = a$ and is denoted by $f'(a)$. It means

- $f'(a) = \displaystyle\lim_{h \to 0} \frac{f(a+h)-f(a)}{h}$.

- In general, *derivative* of $f(x)$ with respect to x, at any value of x, is represented as $f'(x)$ and

$$f'(x) = \lim_{h \to 0} \frac{f(x+h)-f(x)}{h}$$

  This is called First Principle of Derivatives.

  <u>Note</u> that we can use Δx instead of h in the above expression, and hence we can also write it as

$$f'(x) = \lim_{\Delta x \to 0} \frac{f(x+\Delta x)-f(x)}{\Delta x}$$

- $\dfrac{d}{dx}$ denotes derivative with respect to x.

- We can write $f'(x)$ as $\dfrac{d}{dx}\left(f(x)\right)$ and if $y = f(x)$, then $f'(x) = \dfrac{dy}{dx}$.

Derivatives of some important functions are listed from next page, which can easily be obtained by using first principle of derivative and concepts of Limits.

2 Derivatives of some important functions

2.1 Formulae

1) $\dfrac{d}{dx}(x^n) = n\,x^{n-1}$

$\longrightarrow \dfrac{d}{dx}(x) = 1$

$\longrightarrow \dfrac{d}{dx}(k) = 0,$
where k is any constant

$\longrightarrow \dfrac{d}{dx}\left(\dfrac{1}{x}\right) = -\dfrac{1}{x^2}$

2) $\dfrac{d}{dx}(\sin x) = \cos x$

3) $\dfrac{d}{dx}(\cos x) = -\sin x$

4) $\dfrac{d}{dx}(\tan\ x) = \sec^2 x$

5) $\dfrac{d}{dx}(\cot x) = -\csc^2 x$

6) $\dfrac{d}{dx}(\sec x) = \sec x \cdot \tan x$

7) $\dfrac{d}{dx}(\csc x) = -\csc x \cot x$

8) $\dfrac{d}{dx}(e^x) = e^x$

9) $\dfrac{d}{dx}(a^x) = a^x \log a$

10) $\dfrac{d}{dx}(\log x) = \dfrac{1}{x}$

11) $\dfrac{d}{dx}(\log_a x) = \dfrac{1}{x \log a}$

12) $\dfrac{d}{dx}(\sin^{-1}x) = \dfrac{1}{\sqrt{1-x^2}}$

13) $\dfrac{d}{dx}(\cos^{-1}x) = \dfrac{-1}{\sqrt{1-x^2}}$

14) $\dfrac{d}{dx}(\tan^{-1}x) = \dfrac{1}{1+x^2}$

15) $\dfrac{d}{dx}(\cot^{-1}x) = \dfrac{-1}{1+x^2}$

16) $\dfrac{d}{dx}(\sec^{-1}x) = \dfrac{1}{x\sqrt{x^2-1}}$

17) $\dfrac{d}{dx}(\csc^{-1}x) = \dfrac{-1}{x\sqrt{x^2-1}}$

3 Algebra of Derivatives

If the derivatives of two functions $u = f(x)$ and $v = g(x)$ exist in their common domain , then derivatives of their sum and difference also exist in their common domains and are, respectively equal to sum and difference of their derivatives.

But the derivatives of their product and quotient are not the product and quotient of their derivatives.

The rules to find derivatives of sum, difference, product and quotient of 2 functions are as follows:

*Asterisk (*) marked article (if any) is **not** in CBSE 2025-26 syllabus.*

3.1   Sum or Difference Rule

$$\frac{d}{dx}\left[f(x)\pm g(x)\right]=\frac{d}{dx}f(x)\pm\frac{d}{dx}g(x)$$

OR

$$\frac{d}{dx}\left[u\pm v\right]=\frac{d}{dx}(u)\pm\frac{d}{dx}(v)$$

3.2   Product Rule

$$\frac{d}{dx}\left[f(x).g(x)\right]=f(x)\frac{d}{dx}(g(x))+g(x)\frac{d}{dx}(f(x))$$

OR

$$\frac{d}{dx}\left[u.v\right]=u\frac{d}{dx}(v)+v\frac{d}{dx}(u)$$

3.3   Quotient Rule

$$\frac{d}{dx}\left[\frac{f(x)}{g(x)}\right]=\frac{g(x)\frac{d}{dx}f(x)-f(x)\frac{d}{dx}g(x)}{[g(x)]^2}$$

OR

$$\frac{d}{dx}\left[\frac{u}{v}\right]=\frac{v\frac{d}{dx}(u)-u\frac{d}{dx}(v)}{v^2}$$

Chapter-15   *Mathematical Reasoning

1   *Mathematical Statement

A sentence is called a mathematically acceptable statement if it is either true or false but not both.

- Sentences with an exclamation, an order, and a question are not mathematical statements.
- Sentences involving variable time such as "today", "tomorrow" or "yesterday" are not statements.
- Mathematical statements are usually denoted by small letters p, q, r, etc.

2   *Negation of a statement

The denial of a statement is called the negation of the statement.

- Negation of statement p is denoted by $\sim p$, and is read as 'not p'.
- To write the negation of a statement, we can use the phrases like, "It is not the case" or "It is false that". These phrases, completely, denies the given statement without any error.
- If statement p is TRUE , then its negation $\sim p$ is FALSE, and vice-versa.

3   *Compound statements

A statement which is made up of two or more simple statements combined together is known as Compound Statement.

- Each simple statement in the compound statement is called a ***component statement.***
- Compound statement is obtained by combining component statements using some connecting words like "and", "or", "if – then", "if and only if", etc.

3.1   *Compound statements with "And"

Here, two or more simple statements are combined by the word 'And' .

- The compound statement 'p and q' is denoted by $p \wedge q$

- The compound statement with 'And' is true if all its component statements are TRUE.
- The compound statement with 'And' is false if at least one of its component statements is FALSE.

3.2 *Compound statements with "Or"

Here, two or more simple statements are combined by the word 'Or'.

There are two types of 'Or': (i) exclusive 'Or'   (ii) inclusive 'Or'.

(i) **Exclusive 'Or':** The statement in which only one of its component statements can be true, i.e., if one statement is TRUE , then other is necessarily FALSE

(ii) **Inclusive 'Or':** The statement in which both of its component statements can be true simultaneously, i.e., if one statement is TRUE , then other may also be TRUE.

- The compound statement 'p or q' is denoted by $p \vee q$
- The compound statement with 'Or' is true if at least one of its component statements is TRUE.
- The compound statement with 'Or' is false if all of its component statements are FALSE.

3.3 *Quantifiers and Connectives

The phrases like 'There exists', 'For all', 'For every', etc. are known as Quantifiers.

The words like 'And', and 'Or' are known as Connectives.

3.4 *Compound statements with "if – then"

- The compound statement 'if p then q' is denoted by $p \Rightarrow q$, which is read as 'p implies q'.
- A statement **"If p then q"** can be rewritten as
  (i) p implies q
  (ii) p is sufficient condition for q
  (iii) q is necessary condition for p
  (iv) p only if q
  (v) $\sim q$ implies $\sim p$

3.4.1 *Contrapositive and Converse statements

- **Contrapositive** of the statement $p \Rightarrow q$ is the statement $\sim q \Rightarrow \sim p$
- **Converse** of the statement $p \Rightarrow q$ is the statement $q \Rightarrow p$

3.5 *Compound statements with "if and only if"

- The compound statement 'p if and only if q' is combination of two 'if – then' statements with 'And' can be written as 'if p then q And if q then p'.
- The compound statement 'p if and only if q' is denoted by $p \Leftrightarrow q$.
- A statement " **p if and only if q**" can be rewritten as
  (i) q if and only if p
  (ii) p implies q and q implies p
  (iii) p is necessary and sufficient condition for q
  (iv) q is necessary and sufficient condition for p

4 *Validation of statements

A statement is called **valid** statement if it is true, and if it is false, it is called **invalid** statement.

4.1 *Validating statement 'p and q'

To prove that the statement 'p and q' is true, there are following two steps:

Step-1: Show that the statement p is true.

Step-2: Show that the statement q is true.

4.2 *Validating statement 'p or q'

To prove that the statement 'p or q' is true, show that any one of the following two cases is true.

Case 1: By assuming that p is false, show that q must be true.

Case 2: By assuming that q is false, show that p must be true.

4.3 *Validating statement 'if p then q'

To prove that the statement 'if p then q' is true, show that any one of the following two cases is true.

Case 1 (Direct method):

By assuming that p is true, show that q must be true.

Case 2 (Contrapositive method):

By assuming that q is false, show that p must be false.

4.4   *Validating statement *'p if and only if q'*

To prove that the statement 'p if and only if q' is true, there are following two steps:

Step-1: Show that if p is true , then q is true, i.e., show that 'if p then q' is true.

Step-2: Show that if q is true , then p is true, i.e., 'if q then p' is true.

Chapter-16   Statistics

1 Measures of Central Tendency

A data point which may be considered as the representative of whole data is known as Measure of Central Tendency.

- **Mean**, **Mode** and **Median** are 3 *measures of central tendency*.
- They have the same units as that of the given data.

2 Measures of Dispersion

A number which may describe the variability in the given data is known as Measure of Dispersion.

- (i) **Range**, (ii) **Quartile deviation**, (iii) **Mean deviation**, (iv) **Standard deviation** are *measures of dispersion*.
- They have the same units as that of the given data.

3 Range

The difference of maximum and minimum values of given data series is called the Range of the data.

- Range of data = Maximum value – Minimum value.
- The range of data does not tell about the dispersion of the data from a measure of central tendency.

4 Mean Deviation

- Mean deviation may be obtained from any measure of central tendency (i.e., from mean, median or mode).
- The mean deviation from a central tendency is the mean of absolute values of differences of all data points from the given central tendency.

Note: The given data may be Ungrouped Data (or Raw Data) or Grouped Data.

Grouped data can be presented in two ways:

(i) Discrete Frequency Distribution

(ii) Continuous Frequency Distribution.

4.1 Mean Deviation from Mean

4.1.1 Ungrouped Data

Given data : $x_1, \ x_2, \ x_3, \dots , \ x_n$

Number of observations $= N$

- Mean: $\overline{x} = \dfrac{sum\,of\,all\,observations}{Number\,of\,observations} = \dfrac{\displaystyle\sum_{i=1}^{n} x_i}{N}$

- Absolute Deviations from Mean are:

  $|\, x_1 - \bar{x}\,|, |\, x_2 - \bar{x}\,|, |\, x_3 - \bar{x}\,|, \dots , |\, x_n - \bar{x}\,|$

- Mean Deviation from Mean:

$$\text{M.D.}(\,\overline{x}\,) = \frac{\displaystyle\sum_{i=1}^{n} |\, x_i - \bar{x}\,|}{N}$$

4.1.2 Discrete Frequency Distribution

There are 3 methods (a) Direct Method (b) Assumed Mean Method (c) Step-Deviation Method.

(i) Direct Method:

Given data:

Observation (x_i)	x_1	x_2	x_3	.	.	.	x_n
Frequency (f_i)	f_1	f_2	f_3	.	.	.	f_n

Table Formation:

Observation (x_i)	Frequency (f_i)	$f_i\,x_i$	$f_i\,|\,x_i - \overline{x}\,|$
x_1	f_1	-	-
x_2	f_2	-	-
.	.	-	-
.	.	-	-
.	.	-	-
x_n	f_n	-	-
	$\displaystyle\sum_{i=1}^{n} f_i = ?$	$\displaystyle\sum_{i=1}^{n} f_i\, x_i = ?$	$\displaystyle\sum_{i=1}^{n} f_i\,|\,x_i - \bar{x}\,| = ?$

*Asterisk (*) marked article (if any) is **not** in CBSE 2025-26 syllabus.*

Formulae:

- Mean: $\displaystyle \bar{x} = \frac{\sum\limits_{i=1}^{n} f_i x_i}{\sum\limits_{i=1}^{n} f_i}$

- Mean Deviation from Mean:

$$\text{M.D.}(\bar{x}) = \frac{\sum\limits_{i=1}^{n} f_i \,|\, x_i - \bar{x}\,|}{\sum\limits_{i=1}^{n} f_i}$$

(ii) Assumed Mean Method:

Given data:

Observation (x_i)	x_1	x_2	x_3	.	.	.	x_n
Frequency (f_i)	f_1	f_2	f_3	.	.	.	f_n

Table Formation:

Let a = Assumed Mean

$d_i = (x_i - a)$ = Deviations from assumed mean

Observation (x_i)	Frequency (f_i)	$d_i = x_i - a$	$f_i d_i$	$|x_i - \bar{x}|$	$f_i \,|\, x_i - \bar{x}\,|$
x_1	f_1	-	-	-	-
x_2	f_2	-	-	-	-
.	.	-	-	-	-
.	.	-	-	-	-
.	.	-	-	-	-
x_n	f_n	-	-	-	-
	$\sum\limits_{i=1}^{n} f_i = \,?$		$\sum\limits_{i=1}^{n} f_i d_i = \,?$		$\sum\limits_{i=1}^{n} f_i \,|\, x_i - \bar{x}\,| = \,?$

Formulae:

a = Assumed Mean

$d_i = (x_i - a)$ = Deviations from assumed mean

- Mean: $\displaystyle \overline{x} = a + \frac{\sum\limits_{i=1}^{n} f_i d_i}{\sum\limits_{i=1}^{n} f_i}$

- Mean Deviation from Mean:

$$\text{M.D.}(\overline{x}) = \frac{\sum\limits_{i=1}^{n} f_i \, |x_i - \overline{x}|}{\sum\limits_{i=1}^{n} f_i}$$

(iii) Step – Deviation Method:
   Given data:

Observation (x_i)	x_1	x_2	x_3	.	.	.	x_n
Frequency (f_i)	f_1	f_2	f_3	.	.	.	f_n

Table Formation:

Let a = Assumed Mean

$d_i = (x_i - a)$ = Deviations from assumed mean

Common Factor in deviations = h

Step–Deviations, $u_i = \dfrac{x_i - a}{h}$

Observation (x_i)	Frequency (f_i)	$d_i = x_i - a$	$u_i = \dfrac{x_i - a}{h}$	$f_i u_i$	$|x_i - \overline{x}|$	$f_i \, |x_i - \overline{x}|$
x_1	f_1	-	-	-	-	-
x_2	f_2	-	-	-	-	-
.	.	-	-	-	-	-
.	.	-	-	-	-	-
.	.	-	-	-	-	-
x_n	f_n	-	-	-	-	-
	$\sum\limits_{i=1}^{n} f_i = ?$			$\sum\limits_{i=1}^{n} f_i u_i = ?$		$\sum\limits_{i=1}^{n} f_i|x_i - \overline{x}| = ?$

Formulae:

a = Assumed Mean

$d_i = (x_i - a)$ = Deviations from assumed mean

Common Factor in deviations = h

Step – Deviations, $u_i = \dfrac{x_i - a}{h}$

- Mean: $\overline{x} = a + h \cdot \left(\dfrac{\displaystyle\sum_{i=1}^{n} f_i u_i}{\displaystyle\sum_{i=1}^{n} f_i} \right)$

- Mean Deviation from Mean:

$$\text{M.D.}(\overline{x}) = \dfrac{\displaystyle\sum_{i=1}^{n} f_i \,|x_i - \overline{x}|}{\displaystyle\sum_{i=1}^{n} f_i}$$

4.1.3 Continuous Frequency Distribution

There are 3 methods (a) Direct Method (b) Assumed Mean Method (c) Step-Deviation Method.

(i) Direct Method:

Given data:

Class Interval ($l_i - u_i$)	$l_1 - u_1$	$l_2 - u_2$	$l_3 - u_3$	.	.	.	$l_n - u_n$
Frequency (f_i)	f_1	f_2	f_3	.	.	.	f_n

Table Formation:

Class Interval ($l_i - u_i$)	Class Mark $x_i = \dfrac{l_i + u_i}{2}$	Frequency (f_i)	$f_i x_i$	$\|x_i - \overline{x}\|$	$f_i\|x_i - \overline{x}\|$
$l_1 - u_1$	x_1	f_1	-	-	-
$l_2 - u_2$	x_2	f_2	-	-	-
.	.	.	-	-	-
.	.	.	-	-	-
.	.	.	-	-	-
$l_n - u_n$	x_n	f_n	-	-	-
		$\displaystyle\sum_{i=1}^{n} f_i = ?$	$\displaystyle\sum_{i=1}^{n} f_i = ?$		$\displaystyle\sum_{i=1}^{n} f_i\|x_i - \overline{x}\| = ?$

Formulae:

- Class Marks: $x_i = \dfrac{l_i + u_i}{2}$

- Mean: $\bar{x} = \dfrac{\displaystyle\sum_{i=1}^{n} f_i x_i}{\displaystyle\sum_{i=1}^{n} f_i}$

- Mean Deviation from Mean:

$$\text{M.D.}(\bar{x}) = \dfrac{\displaystyle\sum_{i=1}^{n} f_i \,|x_i - \bar{x}|}{\displaystyle\sum_{i=1}^{n} f_i}$$

(ii) Assumed Mean Method:

Given data:

Class Interval ($l_i - u_i$)	$l_1 - u_1$	$l_2 - u_2$	$l_3 - u_3$	.	.	.	$l_n - u_n$
Frequency (f_i)	f_1	f_2	f_3	.	.	.	f_n

Table Formation:

Class Marks, $x_i = \dfrac{l_i + u_i}{2}$

Let a = Assumed Mean

Deviations from assumed mean, $d_i = (x_i - a)$

Class Interval ($l_i - u_i$)	Class Mark $x_i = \dfrac{l_i + u_i}{2}$	Freq (f_i)	$d_i = x_i - a$	$f_i d_i$	$\|x_i - \bar{x}\|$	$f_i\,\|x_i - \bar{x}\|$
$l_1 - u_1$	x_1	f_1	-	-	-	-
$l_2 - u_2$	x_2	f_2	-	-	-	-
.	.	.	-	-	-	-
.	.	.	-	-	-	-
.	.	.	-	-	-	-
$l_n - u_n$	x_n	f_n	-	-	-	-
		$\displaystyle\sum_{i=1}^{n} f_i$ = ?		$\displaystyle\sum_{i=1}^{n} f_i d_i$ =?		$\displaystyle\sum_{i=1}^{n} f_i\,\|x_i - \bar{x}\|$ =?

Formulae:

Class Marks: $\quad x_i = \dfrac{l_i + u_i}{2}$

a = Assumed Mean

$d_i = (x_i - a)$ = Deviations from assumed mean

- Mean: $\bar{x} = a + \dfrac{\sum\limits_{i=1}^{n} f_i d_i}{\sum\limits_{i=1}^{n} f_i}$

- Mean Deviation from Mean:

$$\text{M.D.}(\bar{x}) = \dfrac{\sum\limits_{i=1}^{n} f_i \, |x_i - \bar{x}|}{\sum\limits_{i=1}^{n} f_i}$$

(iii) Step – Deviation Method:

Given data:

Class Interval ($l_i - u_i$)	$l_1 - u_1$	$l_2 - u_2$	$l_3 - u_3$	.	.	.	$l_n - u_n$
Frequency (f_i)	f_1	f_2	f_3	.	.	.	f_n

Table Formation:

Class Marks: $\quad x_i = \dfrac{l_i + u_i}{2}$

Let a = Assumed Mean

Deviations from assumed mean, $d_i = (x_i - a)$

Common Factor in deviations, $= h$

Step – Deviations, $u_i = \dfrac{x_i - a}{h}$

Class Interval $(l_i - u_i)$	Class Mark $x_i = \dfrac{l_i+u_i}{2}$	Freq (f_i)	$d_i = x_i - a$	$u_i = \dfrac{x_i-a}{h}$	$f_i\, u_i$	$|x_i - \bar{x}|$	$f_i\,|x_i - \bar{x}|$
$l_1 - u_1$	x_1	f_1	-	-	-	-	-
$l_2 - u_2$	x_2	f_2	-	-	-	-	-
.	.	.	-	-	-	-	-
.	.	.	-	-	-	-	-
.	.	.	-	-	-	-	-
$l_n - u_n$	x_n	f_n	-	-	-	-	-
		$\displaystyle\sum_{i=1}^{n} f_i = ?$			$\displaystyle\sum_{i=1}^{n} f_i u_i = ?$		$\displaystyle\sum_{i=1}^{n} f_i\,|x_i - \bar{x}| = ?$

Formulae:

Class Marks: $\qquad x_i = \dfrac{l_i+u_i}{2}$

a = Assumed Mean

$d_i = (x_i - a)$ = Deviations from assumed mean

Common Factor in deviations = h

Step – Deviations, $u_i = \dfrac{x_i-a}{h}$

- Mean: $\bar{x} = a + h\cdot\left(\dfrac{\displaystyle\sum_{i=1}^{n} f_i u_i}{\displaystyle\sum_{i=1}^{n} f_i}\right)$

- Mean Deviation from Mean:

$$\text{M.D.}(\bar{x}) = \dfrac{\displaystyle\sum_{i=1}^{n} f_i\,|x_i - \bar{x}|}{\displaystyle\sum_{i=1}^{n} f_i}$$

*Asterisk (*) marked article (if any) is **not** in CBSE 2025-26 syllabus.*

4.2 Mean Deviation from Median

4.2.1 Ungrouped Data

Given data (in ascending order) : $x_1, \ x_2, \ x_3, \ldots, \ x_n$

Number of observations $= N$

- If N is odd , then

  Median: $M = \left(\dfrac{N+1}{2}\right)^{th}$ observation

- If N is even , then

  Median: $M = \dfrac{\left(\frac{N}{2}\right)^{th} observation + \left(\frac{N+1}{2}\right)^{th} observation}{2}$

- Absolute Deviations from Median are:
  $|x_1 - M|, \ |x_2 - M|, \ |x_3 - M|, \ldots, |x_n - M|$

- Mean Deviation from Median:

  $$M.D.(M) = \frac{\sum\limits_{i=1}^{n}|x_i - M|}{N}$$

4.2.2 Discrete Frequency Distribution

Given data:

Observation (x_i)	x_1	x_2	x_3	.	.	.	x_n
Frequency (f_i)	f_1	f_2	f_3	.	.	.	f_n

Table Formation:

Observation (x_i)	Freq (f_i)	Cum. Frequency (cf_i)	$f_i\,|x_i - M|$	$f_i\,|x_i - M|$
x_1	f_1	f_1	-	-
x_2	f_2	$f_1 + f_2$	-	-
.	.	$f_1 + f_2 + f_3$	-	-
.	.	.	-	-
.	.	.	-	-
x_n	f_n	$f_1 + f_2 + f_3 \ldots + f_n$	-	-
	$\sum\limits_{i=1}^{n} f_i = \ ?$			$\sum\limits_{i=1}^{n} f_i\,|x_i - M| = ?$

Formulae:

Number of observations, $\quad N = \sum_{i=1}^{n} f_i$

- If N is odd, then

  Mark the row in the table which contains $\left(\frac{N+1}{2}\right)^{th}$ observation in cf_i column.

  Median: $\quad M = \left(\frac{N+1}{2}\right)^{th}$ observation

- If N is even, then

  Mark the rows in the table which contain $\left(\frac{N}{2}\right)^{th}$ observation and $\left(\frac{N+1}{2}\right)^{th}$ observation in cf_i column.

  Median: $\quad M = \dfrac{\left(\frac{N}{2}\right)^{th} observation + \left(\frac{N+1}{2}\right)^{th} observation}{2}$

- Absolute Deviations from Median are:
  $| x_1 - M |, \ | x_2 - M |, \ | x_3 - M |, \ldots, | x_n - M |$

- Mean Deviation from Median:

$$\text{M.D.}(M) = \dfrac{\sum\limits_{i=1}^{n} f_i \, | x_i - M |}{\sum\limits_{i=1}^{n} f_i}$$

4.2.3 Continuous Frequency Distribution

Given data:

Class Interval ($l_i - u_i$)	$l_1 - u_1$	$l_2 - u_2$	$l_3 - u_3$	.	.	.	$l_n - u_n$
Frequency (f_i)	f_1	f_2	f_3	.	.	.	f_n

Table Formation:

Class Marks, $x_i = \dfrac{l_i + u_i}{2}$

Class Interval $(l_i - u_i)$	Class Mark $x_i = \dfrac{l_i + u_i}{2}$	Frequency (f_i)	Cumulative Frequency (cf_i)	$\lvert x_i - M \rvert$	$f_i \lvert x_i - M \rvert$
$l_1 - u_1$	x_1	f_1	f_1	-	-
$l_2 - u_2$	x_2	f_2	$f_1 + f_2$	-	-
.	.	.	$f_1 + f_2 + f_3$	-	-
.	.	.	.	-	-
.	.	.	.	-	-
$l_n - u_n$	x_n	f_n	$f_1 + f_2 + f_3 \ldots + f_n$	-	-
		$\displaystyle\sum_{i=1}^{n} f_i = ?$			$\displaystyle\sum_{i=1}^{n} f_i \lvert x_i - M \rvert = ?$

Formulae:

Class Marks:
$$x_i = \frac{l_i + u_i}{2}$$

Number of observations, $N = \displaystyle\sum_{i=1}^{n} f_i$

Half of number of observations $= \dfrac{N}{2}$

Mark median class in the table which contains $\left(\dfrac{N}{2}\right)^{th}$ observation in cf_i column.

$\therefore$ Median class is $= l - u$

Lower limit of median class $= l$

Class size of median class $= h$

Frequency of median class $= f$

Cumulative Frequency of Pre median class $= cf$

- Median:
$$M = l + h \cdot \left(\frac{\dfrac{N}{2} - cf}{f}\right)$$

- Mean Deviation from Median:
$$M.D.(M) = \frac{\displaystyle\sum_{i=1}^{n} \lvert x_i - M \rvert}{N}$$

5   Standard Deviation and Variance

5.1   Ungrouped Data

There are 2 methods: (i) conceptual method (ii) Alternative method (modified form of 1st method)

(i) Conceptual method:

Given data : $x_1, x_2, x_3, \ldots, x_n$

Number of observations = N

- Mean: $\bar{x} = \dfrac{sum\,of\,all\,observations}{Number\,of\,observations} = \dfrac{\sum\limits_{i=1}^{n} x_i}{N}$

- Square of Deviations from Mean are:
$(x_1 - \bar{x})^2, (x_2 - \bar{x})^2, (x_3 - \bar{x})^2, \ldots, (x_n - \bar{x})^2$

- Variance: $\sigma^2 = \dfrac{\sum\limits_{i=1}^{n}(x_i - \bar{x})^2}{N}$

- Standard Deviation: $\sigma = \sqrt{\dfrac{\sum\limits_{i=1}^{n}(x_i - \bar{x})^2}{N}}$

(ii) Alternative method:

Given data : $x_1, x_2, x_3, \ldots, x_n$

Number of observations = N

- Square of observations are:
$(x_1)^2, (x_2)^2, (x_3)^2, \ldots, (x_n)^2$

- Variance:

$$\sigma^2 = \dfrac{\sum\limits_{i=1}^{n}(x_i)^2}{N} - \left(\dfrac{\sum\limits_{i=1}^{n}(x_i)}{N} \right)^2$$

$$\text{OR} \quad \sigma^2 = \dfrac{\sum\limits_{i=1}^{n}(x_i)^2}{N} - (\bar{x})^2$$

*Asterisk (*) marked article (if any) is **not** in CBSE 2025-26 syllabus.*

- Standard Deviation:

$$\sigma = \sqrt{\dfrac{\sum\limits_{i=1}^{n}(x_i)^2}{N} - \left(\dfrac{\sum\limits_{i=1}^{n}(x_i)}{N}\right)^2}$$

$$\text{OR} \quad \sigma = \sqrt{\dfrac{\sum\limits_{i=1}^{n}(x_i)^2}{N} - (\bar{x})^2}$$

5.2 Discrete Frequency Distribution

There are 3 methods (A) Direct Method (B) Assumed Mean Method (C) Step-Deviation Method.

For each of these, we have 2 methods: (i) conceptual method (ii) alternative method.

5.2.1 (A) Direct Method

Given data:

Observation (x_i)	x_1	x_2	x_3	.	.	.	x_n
Frequency (f_i)	f_1	f_2	f_3	.	.	.	f_n

(i) Conceptual method:

Table Formation:

Observation (x_i)	Frequency (f_i)	$f_i x_i$	$f_i (x_i - \bar{x})^2$
x_1	f_1	-	-
x_2	f_2	-	-
.	.	-	-
.	.	-	-
.	.	-	-
x_n	f_n	-	-
	$\sum\limits_{i=1}^{n} f_i = ?$	$\sum\limits_{i=1}^{n} f_i x_i = ?$	$\sum\limits_{i=1}^{n} f_i (x_i - \bar{x})^2 = ?$

*Asterisk (*) marked article (if any) is **not** in CBSE 2025-26 syllabus.*

Formulae:

- Mean:
$$\overline{x} = \frac{\displaystyle\sum_{i=1}^{n} f_i x_i}{\displaystyle\sum_{i=1}^{n} f_i}$$

- Variance:
$$\sigma^2 = \frac{\displaystyle\sum_{i=1}^{n} f_i \left(x_i - \overline{x}\right)^2}{\displaystyle\sum_{i=1}^{n} f_i}$$

- Standard Deviation:
$$\sigma = \sqrt{\frac{\displaystyle\sum_{i=1}^{n} f_i \left(x_i - \overline{x}\right)^2}{\displaystyle\sum_{i=1}^{n} f_i}}$$

(ii) Alternative method:

Table Formation:

Observation (x_i)	Frequency (f_i)	$f_i x_i$	$f_i x_i^2$
x_1	f_1	-	-
x_2	f_2	-	-
.	.	-	-
.	.	-	-
.	.	-	-
x_n	f_n	-	-
	$\displaystyle\sum_{i=1}^{n} f_i = ?$	$\displaystyle\sum_{i=1}^{n} f_i x_i = ?$	$\displaystyle\sum_{i=1}^{n} f_i x_i^2 = ?$

Formulae:

- Mean:
$$\overline{x} = \frac{\displaystyle\sum_{i=1}^{n} f_i x_i}{\displaystyle\sum_{i=1}^{n} f_i}$$

---

*Asterisk (*) marked article (if any) is **not** in CBSE 2025-26 syllabus.*

- Variance:

$$\sigma^2 = \frac{\sum\limits_{i=1}^{n} f_i x_i^2}{\sum\limits_{i=1}^{n} f_i} - \left(\frac{\sum\limits_{i=1}^{n} f_i x_i}{\sum\limits_{i=1}^{n} f_i} \right)^2$$

OR

$$\sigma^2 = \frac{\sum\limits_{i=1}^{n} f_i x_i^2}{\sum\limits_{i=1}^{n} f_i} - (\bar{x})^2$$

- Standard Deviation:

$$\sigma = \sqrt{\frac{\sum\limits_{i=1}^{n} f_i x_i^2}{\sum\limits_{i=1}^{n} f_i} - \left(\frac{\sum\limits_{i=1}^{n} f_i x_i}{\sum\limits_{i=1}^{n} f_i} \right)^2}$$

OR

$$\sigma = \sqrt{\frac{\sum\limits_{i=1}^{n} f_i x_i^2}{\sum\limits_{i=1}^{n} f_i} - (\bar{x})^2}$$

5.2.2 (B) Assumed Mean Method

Given data:

Observation (x_i)	x_1	x_2	x_3	.	.	.	x_n
Frequency (f_i)	f_1	f_2	f_3	.	.	.	f_n

Table Formation:

Let a = Assumed Mean

$d_i = (x_i - a)$ = Deviations from assumed mean

Observation (x_i)	Frequency (f_i)	$d_i = x_i - a$	$f_i d_i$	$f_i d_i^2$
x_1	f_1	-	-	-
x_2	f_2	-	-	-
.	.	-	-	-
.	.	-	-	-
.	.	-	-	-
x_n	f_n	-	-	-
	$\sum\limits_{i=1}^{n} f_i = ?$		$\sum\limits_{i=1}^{n} f_i d_i = ?$	$\sum\limits_{i=1}^{n} f_i d_i^2 = ?$

*Asterisk (*) marked article (if any) is **not** in CBSE 2025-26 syllabus.*

Formulae:

a = Assumed Mean

$d_i = (x_i - a)$ = Deviations from assumed mean

- Mean: $\bar{x} = a + \dfrac{\sum\limits_{i=1}^{n} f_i d_i}{\sum\limits_{i=1}^{n} f_i}$

- Variance: $\sigma^2 = \dfrac{\sum\limits_{i=1}^{n} f_i d_i^2}{\sum\limits_{i=1}^{n} f_i} - \left(\dfrac{\sum\limits_{i=1}^{n} f_i d_i}{\sum\limits_{i=1}^{n} f_i}\right)^2$

- Standard Deviation:

$$\sigma = \sqrt{\dfrac{\sum\limits_{i=1}^{n} f_i d_i^2}{\sum\limits_{i=1}^{n} f_i} - \left(\dfrac{\sum\limits_{i=1}^{n} f_i d_i}{\sum\limits_{i=1}^{n} f_i}\right)^2}$$

5.2.3 (C) Step – Deviation Method

Given data:

Observation (x_i)	x_1	x_2	x_3	.	.	.	x_n
Frequency (f_i)	f_1	f_2	f_3	.	.	.	f_n

Table Formation:

Let a = Assumed Mean

$d_i = (x_i - a)$ = Deviations from assumed mean

Common Factor in deviations $= h$

Step – Deviations, $u_i = \dfrac{x_i - a}{h}$

Observation (x_i)	Freq (f_i)	$d_i = x_i - a$	$u_i = \dfrac{x_i - a}{h}$	$f_i u_i$	$f_i u_i^2$
x_1	f_1	-	-	-	-
x_2	f_2	-	-	-	-
.	.	-	-	-	-
.	.	-	-	-	-
.	.	-	-	-	-
x_n	f_n	-	-	-	-
	$\sum\limits_{i=1}^{n} f_i = ?$			$\sum\limits_{i=1}^{n} f_i u_i = ?$	$\sum\limits_{i=1}^{n} f_i u_i^2 = ?$

Formulae:

a = Assumed Mean

$d_i = (x_i - a) =$ Deviations from assumed mean

Common Factor in deviations = h

Step – Deviations, $u_i = \dfrac{x_i - a}{h}$

- Mean: $\bar{x} = a + h \cdot \left(\dfrac{\sum\limits_{i=1}^{n} f_i u_i}{\sum\limits_{i=1}^{n} f_i} \right)$

- Variance:

$$\sigma^2 = h^2 \cdot \left[\dfrac{\sum\limits_{i=1}^{n} f_i u_i^{\,2}}{\sum\limits_{i=1}^{n} f_i} - \left(\dfrac{\sum\limits_{i=1}^{n} f_i u_i}{\sum\limits_{i=1}^{n} f_i} \right)^2 \right]$$

- Standard Deviation:

$$\sigma = h \cdot \sqrt{ \left[\dfrac{\sum\limits_{i=1}^{n} f_i u_i^{\,2}}{\sum\limits_{i=1}^{n} f_i} - \left(\dfrac{\sum\limits_{i=1}^{n} f_i u_i}{\sum\limits_{i=1}^{n} f_i} \right)^2 \right] }$$

5.3 Continuous Frequency Distribution

There are 3 methods (A) Direct Method (B) Assumed Mean Method (C) Step-Deviation Method.

For each of these we have 2 methods: (i) conceptual method (ii) alternative method.

5.3.1 (A) Direct Method

Given data:

Class Interval $(l_i - u_i)$	$l_1 - u_1$	$l_2 - u_2$	$l_3 - u_3$	.	.	.	$l_n - u_n$
Frequency (f_i)	f_1	f_2	f_3	.	.	.	f_n

(i) conceptual method:

Table Formation:

Class Marks, $x_i = \dfrac{l_i + u_i}{2}$

Class Interval $(l_i - u_i)$	Class Mark $x_i = \dfrac{l_i + u_i}{2}$	Freq (f_i)	$f_i x_i$	$f_i(x_i - \bar{x})^2$
$l_1 - u_1$	x_1	f_1	-	-
$l_2 - u_2$	x_2	f_2	-	-
.	.	.	-	-
.	.	.	-	-
.	.	.	-	-
$l_n - u_n$	x_n	f_n	-	-
		$\displaystyle\sum_{i=1}^{n} f_i = ?$	$\displaystyle\sum_{i=1}^{n} f_i x_i = ?$	$\displaystyle\sum_{i=1}^{n} f_i(x_i - \bar{x})^2 = ?$

Formulae:

- Mean:
$$\bar{x} = \frac{\displaystyle\sum_{i=1}^{n} f_i x_i}{\displaystyle\sum_{i=1}^{n} f_i}$$

- Variance:
$$\sigma^2 = \frac{\displaystyle\sum_{i=1}^{n} f_i(x_i - \bar{x})^2}{\displaystyle\sum_{i=1}^{n} f_i}$$

- Standard Deviation:
$$\sigma = \sqrt{\frac{\displaystyle\sum_{i=1}^{n} f_i(x_i - \bar{x})^2}{\displaystyle\sum_{i=1}^{n} f_i}}$$

(ii) Alternative method:
Table Formation:

Class Interval $(l_i - u_i)$	Class Mark $x_i = \dfrac{l_i + u_i}{2}$	Frequency (f_i)	$f_i x_i$	$f_i x_i^2$
$l_1 - u_1$	x_1	f_1	-	-
$l_2 - u_2$	x_2	f_2	-	-
.	.	.	-	-
.	.	.	-	-
.	.	.	-	-
$l_n - u_n$	x_n	f_n	-	-
		$\displaystyle\sum_{i=1}^{n} f_i = ?$	$\displaystyle\sum_{i=1}^{n} f_i x_i = ?$	$\displaystyle\sum_{i=1}^{n} f_i x_i^2 = ?$

---

*Asterisk (*) marked article (if any) is **not** in CBSE 2025-26 syllabus.*

Formulae:

- Mean:

$$\bar{x} = \frac{\displaystyle\sum_{i=1}^{n} f_i x_i}{\displaystyle\sum_{i=1}^{n} f_i}$$

- Variance:

$$\sigma^2 = \frac{\displaystyle\sum_{i=1}^{n} f_i x_i^{\,2}}{\displaystyle\sum_{i=1}^{n} f_i} - \left(\frac{\displaystyle\sum_{i=1}^{n} f_i x_i}{\displaystyle\sum_{i=1}^{n} f_i} \right)^{2}$$

OR

$$\sigma^2 = \frac{\displaystyle\sum_{i=1}^{n} f_i x_i^{\,2}}{\displaystyle\sum_{i=1}^{n} f_i} - \left(\bar{x} \right)^{2}$$

- Standard Deviation:

$$\sigma = \sqrt{\frac{\displaystyle\sum_{i=1}^{n} f_i x_i^{\,2}}{\displaystyle\sum_{i=1}^{n} f_i} - \left(\frac{\displaystyle\sum_{i=1}^{n} f_i x_i}{\displaystyle\sum_{i=1}^{n} f_i} \right)^{2}}$$

OR

$$\sigma = \sqrt{\frac{\displaystyle\sum_{i=1}^{n} f_i x_i^{\,2}}{\displaystyle\sum_{i=1}^{n} f_i} - \left(\bar{x} \right)^{2}}$$

5.3.2 (B) Assumed Mean Method

Given data:

Class Interval $(l_i - u_i)$	$l_1 - u_1$	$l_2 - u_2$	$l_3 - u_3$	.	.	.	$l_n - u_n$
Frequency (f_i)	f_1	f_2	f_3	.	.	.	f_n

*Asterisk (*) marked article (if any) is **not** in CBSE 2025-26 syllabus.*

Table Formation:

Let a = Assumed Mean

$d_i = (x_i - a)$ = Deviations from assumed mean

Class Interval ($l_i - u_i$)	Class Mark $x_i = \frac{l_i + u_i}{2}$	Frequency (f_i)	$d_i = x_i - a$	$f_i d_i$	$f_i d_i^2$
$l_1 - u_1$	x_1	f_1	-	-	-
$l_2 - u_2$	x_2	f_2	-	-	-
.	.	.	-	-	-
.	.	.	-	-	-
.	.	.	-	-	-
$l_n - u_n$	x_n	f_n	-	-	-
		$\sum_{i=1}^{n} f_i = ?$		$\sum_{i=1}^{n} f_i d_i = ?$	$\sum_{i=1}^{n} f_i d_i^2 = ?$

Formulae:

a = Assumed Mean

$d_i = (x_i - a)$ = Deviations from assumed mean

- Mean:

$$\overline{x} = a + \frac{\sum_{i=1}^{n} f_i d_i}{\sum_{i=1}^{n} f_i}$$

- Variance:

$$\sigma^2 = \frac{\sum_{i=1}^{n} f_i d_i^2}{\sum_{i=1}^{n} f_i} - \left(\frac{\sum_{i=1}^{n} f_i d_i}{\sum_{i=1}^{n} f_i} \right)^2$$

- Standard Deviation:

$$\sigma = \sqrt{\frac{\sum_{i=1}^{n} f_i d_i^2}{\sum_{i=1}^{n} f_i} - \left(\frac{\sum_{i=1}^{n} f_i d_i}{\sum_{i=1}^{n} f_i} \right)^2}$$

*Asterisk (*) marked article (if any) is **not** in CBSE 2025-26 syllabus.*

5.3.3 (C) Step – Deviation Method

Given data:

Class Interval ($l_i - u_i$)	$l_1 - u_1$	$l_2 - u_2$	$l_3 - u_3$	.	.	.	$l_n - u_n$
Frequency (f_i)	f_1	f_2	f_3	.	.	.	f_n

Table Formation:

Let a = Assumed Mean

$d_i = (x_i - a)$ = Deviations from assumed mean

Common Factor in deviation = h

Step – Deviations, $u_i = \dfrac{x_i - a}{h}$

Class Interval ($l_i - u_i$)	Class Mark $x_i = \dfrac{l_i + u_i}{2}$	Frequency (f_i)	$d_i = x_i - a$	$u_i = \dfrac{x_i - a}{h}$	$f_i u_i$	$f_i u_i^2$
$l_1 - u_1$	x_1	f_1	-	-	-	-
$l_2 - u_2$	x_2	f_2	-	-	-	-
.	.	.	-	-	-	-
.	.	.	-	-	-	-
.	.	.	-	-	-	-
$l_n - u_n$	x_n	f_n	-	-	-	-
		$\displaystyle\sum_{i=1}^{n} f_i = ?$			$\displaystyle\sum_{i=1}^{n} f_i u_i = ?$	$\displaystyle\sum_{i=1}^{n} f_i u_i^2 = ?$

Formulae:

a = Assumed Mean

$d_i = (x_i - a)$ = Deviations from assumed mean

Common Factor in deviations = h

Step – Deviations, $u_i = \dfrac{x_i - a}{h}$

- Mean:

$$\overline{x} = a + h \cdot \left(\dfrac{\sum\limits_{i=1}^{n} f_i u_i}{\sum\limits_{i=1}^{n} f_i} \right)$$

- Variance:

$$\sigma^2 = h^2 \cdot \left[\dfrac{\sum\limits_{i=1}^{n} f_i u_i^{\,2}}{\sum\limits_{i=1}^{n} f_i} - \left(\dfrac{\sum\limits_{i=1}^{n} f_i u_i}{\sum\limits_{i=1}^{n} f_i} \right)^2 \right]$$

- Standard Deviation:

$$\sigma = h \cdot \sqrt{\left[\dfrac{\sum\limits_{i=1}^{n} f_i u_i^{\,2}}{\sum\limits_{i=1}^{n} f_i} - \left(\dfrac{\sum\limits_{i=1}^{n} f_i u_i}{\sum\limits_{i=1}^{n} f_i} \right)^2 \right]}$$

6   *Coefficient of Variation

The measure of variability which is independent of units is called *coefficient of variation* (denoted as C.V.).

$$\textbf{C.V.} = \dfrac{\sigma}{\overline{x}} \times \textbf{100}$$

- It is used to compare variability in different series of data, especially data with different units where we cannot use Measures of Dispersion.

*Asterisk (*) marked article (if any) is **not** in CBSE 2025-26 syllabus.*

Chapter-17   Probability

1 Random Experiment

An experiment is called random experiment if it satisfies the following two conditions:

(i) It has more than one possible result (outcome).
(ii) It is not possible to predict the outcome in advance.

2 Sample Space and Sample Points

- The set of all possible outcomes of a random experiment is called the *sample space* of the experiment. Sample space is denoted by the symbol S.
- Each outcome of the random experiment or each element of the sample space is called *sample point*.

3 Sample space for tossing a coin

(i) A Coin tossed one time: S = { H,T}
Number of elements = 2.   It is denoted as $n(S) = 2$

(ii) A Coin tossed two times: S = { HH,HT,TH,TT}
Number of elements = 4. $n(S) = 4$

(iii) A Coin tossed three times:
S = {HHH,HHT,HTH,HTT,THH,THT,TTH,TTT}

Number of elements = 8. It is denoted as $n(S) = 8$

(iv) A Coin tossed four times:
S= {HHHH,HHHT,HHTH,HHTT,HTHH,HTHT,HTTH,HTTT,

THHH,THHT,THTH,THTT,TTHH,TTHT,TTTH,TTTT}

Number of elements = 16. It is denoted as $n(S) = 16$

- In general, $n(S) = 2^p$, where p = number of times a coin is tossed or number of coins tossed one time.

4 Sample space for throwing a dice

(i) A dice thrown one time: S = {1,2,3,4,5,6}
Number of elements = 6.   It is denoted as $n(S) = 6$

(ii) A dice thrown two times:

$$S = \{(1,1),(1,2),(1,3),(1,4),(1,5),(1,6),$$

$$(2,1),(2,2),(2,3),(2,4),(2,5),(2,6),$$

$$(3,1),(3,2),(3,3),(3,4),(3,5),(3,6),$$

$$(4,1),(4,2),(4,3),(4,4),(4,5),(4,6),$$

$$(5,1),(5,2),(5,3),(5,4),(5,5),(5,6),$$

$$(6,1),(6,2),(6,3),(6,4),(6,5),(6,6),\}$$

Number of elements = 36. $n(S) = 36$

(iii) A dice thrown three times:

Sample space is S=

$\{(1,1,1),\ldots,(1,1,6),(1,2,1),\ldots,(1,2,6),(1,3,1),\ldots,(1,3,6),(1,4,1),\ldots,$
$(1,4,6),(1,5,1),\ldots,(1,5,1),(1,6,1),\ldots,(1,6,6),$

$(2,1,1),\ldots,(2,1,6),(2,2,1),\ldots,(2,2,6),(2,3,1),\ldots,(2,3,6),(2,4,1),$
$\ldots,(2,4,6),(2,5,1),\ldots,(2,5,1),(2,6,1),\ldots,(2,6,6),$

$(3,1,1),\ldots,(3,1,6),(3,2,1),\ldots,(3,2,6),(3,3,1),\ldots,(3,3,6),(3,4,1),$
$\ldots,(3,4,6),(3,5,1),\ldots,(3,5,1),(3,6,1),\ldots,(3,6,6),$

$(4,1,1),\ldots,(4,1,6),(4,2,1),\ldots,(4,2,6),(4,3,1),\ldots,(4,3,6),(4,4,1),$
$\ldots,(4,4,6),(4,5,1),\ldots,(4,5,1),(4,6,1),\ldots(4,6,6),$

$(5,1,1),\ldots,(5,1,6),(5,2,1),\ldots,(5,2,6),(5,3,1),\ldots,(5,3,6),(5,4,1),$
$\ldots,(5,4,6),(5,5,1),\ldots,(5,5,1),(5,6,1),\ldots,(5,6,6),$

$(6,1,1),\ldots,(6,1,6),(6,2,1),\ldots,(6,2,6),(6,3,1),\ldots,(6,3,6),(6,4,1),$
$\ldots,(6,4,6),(6,5,1),\ldots,(6,5,1),(6,6,1),\ldots,(6,6,6)\}$

Number of elements = 216. $n(S) = 216$

- In general, $n(S) = 6^p$, where p = number of times a dice is thrown or number of dice thrown one time.

5 Event

- Any subset E of a sample space S is called an *event*.
- The number of elements in an event E are denoted as $n(E)$
- The number of events possible are 2^p , where p = number of elements in sample space.

---

6   Types of Events

On the basis of number of elements in an event we can classify events as: Impossible event, Sure event, Simple event, Compound event.

(i) *Impossible event*: An event which cannot occur in the given random experiment is *impossible event*. Number of elements present in this event is 0. It is denoted by empty set $\phi = \{\}$

(ii) *Sure event:* An event which is sure to occur in the given random experiment is *sure event*. Number of elements present in this event is equal to the number of elements in the sample space S. Thus, sample space S denotes sure event.

(iii) *Simple event (or elementary events):* If there is only one outcome (sample point) which is favourable to an event , then it is called as *simple or elementary event*.

  - In a sample space of n elements there are exactly n simple events, each corresponding to an individual element of the sample space.

(iv) *Compound event:* If there are more than one outcome (sample point) which are favourable to an event , then it is called as *compound event*.

7   Algebra of Events

(i) *Event 'not A':* Let the set A denotes an event A in a sample space S of a random experiment. Whenever the outcome of the experiment is not present in set A, we say that the event 'not A' has occurred. The outcomes favourable to the event 'not A' are represented by the set A' or A^c (complement of A).
  - Thus, the event 'not A' = A'
  - $A' = \{\omega: \omega \in S \text{ and } \omega \notin A\}$
  - $A' = S - A$

(ii) *Event 'A or B':* Let the set A and set B denote two events A and B, respectively in a sample space S of a random experiment. Whenever the outcome of the experiment is present in either set A or set B or in both, we say that the event 'A or B' has occurred. The outcomes favourable to the event 'A or B' are represented by the set $A \cup B$ (union of A and B).
  - Thus, the event 'A or B' = $A \cup B$.
  - $A \cup B = \{\omega: \omega \in A \text{ or } \omega \in B\}$

*Asterisk (*) marked article (if any) is **not** in CBSE 2025-26 syllabus.*

(iii) ***Event 'A and B':*** Let the set A and set B denote two events A and B, respectively in a sample space S of a random experiment. Whenever the outcome of the experiment is present in both the sets A and B, we say that the event 'A and B' has occurred. The outcomes favourable to the event 'A and B' are represented by the set $A \cap B$ (intersection of A and B).

- Thus, the event 'A and B' = $A \cap B$.
- $A \cap B = \{\omega : \omega \in A \text{ and } \omega \in B\}$

(iv) ***Event 'A but not B':*** Let the set A and set B denote two events A and B, respectively in a sample space S of a random experiment. Whenever the outcome of the experiment is present in the set A, but it is not present in B, we say that the event 'A but not B' has occurred. The outcomes favourable to the event 'A but not B' are represented by the set A–B (Difference of A and B).

- Thus, the event 'A but not B' = A–B.
- $A-B = \{\omega : \omega \in A \text{ and } \omega \notin B\}$
- $A-B = A \cap B'$

8 Exhaustive Events

Two or more events are said to be *exhaustive events* if at least one of them is sure to occur in the random experiment.

It means if union of sets representing two or more events is sample space S , then these events are called *exhaustive events*.

- If $A \cup B = S$, then events A and B are exhaustive events.
- If $A \cup B \cup C = S$, then events A , B and C are exhaustive events.
- If $E_1 \cup E_2 \cup E_3 \cup ... \cup E_n = S$, then events $E_1, E_2, E_3, ...,E_n$ are exhaustive events.

9 Mutually Exclusive Events

Two or more events are said to be *mutually exclusive events* if no two of them can occur simultaneously.

It means occurrence of one of these events excludes the occurrence of rest of them. Also, it means that if events are disjoint pairwise , then they are *mutually exclusive events*.

- If $A \cap B = \phi$, then events A and B are mutually exclusive events.
- If $A \cap B = \phi$, $B \cap C = \phi$, and $C \cap A = \phi$, then events A , B and C are mutually exclusive events.

---

*Asterisk (*) marked article (if any) is **not** in CBSE 2025-26 syllabus.*

- If $E_i \cap E_j = \phi$ for all $i \neq j$, then all the events $E_1, E_2, E_3, \ldots, E_n$ are mutually exclusive events.
- Simple (or elementary) events from a sample space are always mutually exclusive events.

10 Mutually Exclusive and Exhaustive Events

Two or more events are said to be *mutually exclusive and exhaustive events* if no two them can occur simultaneously and at least one of them is sure to occur.

It means that if events are disjoint pairwise (i.e., intersection is empty set pairwise) and union of all taken together constitute complete sample space S, then they are *mutually exclusive and exhaustive events*.

- If $A \cap B = \phi$ and $A \cup B = S$, then events A and B are mutually exclusive and exhaustive events.
- If $A \cap B = \phi$, $B \cap C = \phi$ and $C \cap A = \phi$, and $A \cup B \cup C = S$, then events A, B and C are mutually exclusive and exhaustive events.
- If $E_i \cap E_j = \phi$ for all $i \neq j$ and $E_1 \cup E_2 \cup E_3 \cup \ldots \cup E_n = S$, then the events $E_1, E_2, E_3, \ldots, E_n$ are mutually exclusive and exhaustive events.

11 Axiomatic Definition of Probability

In a sample space S of a random experiment, the probability, P is a real valued function whose domain is the power set of S, and range is the interval $[0,1]$.

From this definition it follows that minimum possible probability of any event E is 0, and maximum is 1.

We denote probability of any event E as P(E).

11.1 Axioms of Probability

(i) For any event E, $P(E) \geq 0$
(ii) $P(S) = 1$
(iii) If E and F are mutually exclusive events, then
$$P(E \cup F) = P(E) + P(F).$$

*Asterisk (*) marked article (if any) is **not** in CBSE 2025-26 syllabus.*

11.2 Conditions to assign Probabilities

If S be the sample space of a random experiment with n number of sample points, then S = $\{\omega_1, \omega_2, \omega_3, ... \omega_n\}$.

From the axiomatic definition of probability, the following conditions should hold while assigning probabilities:

(i) $0 \leq P(\omega_i) \leq 1$ for each $\omega_i \in S$

(where $P(\omega_i)$ denotes probability of simple event $\{\omega_i\}$)

It means that probability of occurrence of each sample point lies in the interval $[0,1]$

(ii) $P(\omega_1) + P(\omega_2) + ... + P(\omega_n) = 1$

It means that the sum of probabilities of occurrence of each sample point = 1

11.3 Other condition that follows from Axioms

- For any event A, $P(A) = \Sigma P(\omega_i)$, where $\omega_i \in A$.

  It means that probability of occurrence of any event = sum of the probabilities of occurrence of each sample point which belongs to event A.
- $P(\phi) = 0$. It means probability of impossible event = 0

11.4 Probabilities for equally likely outcomes

- Probability of each sample point is $P(\omega_i) = \dfrac{1}{n}$

  where n is number of sample points in the sample space,

  S = $\{\omega_1, \omega_2, \omega_3, ... \omega_n\}$

- For a random experiment of equally likely outcomes, the probability of any event E is given by

  $$P(E) = \frac{Number\ of\ outcomes\ favourable\ to\ E}{Total\ Number\ of\ outcomes}$$

  or $P(E) = \dfrac{n(E)}{n(S)}$

  where, $n(E)$ denotes number of elements in event E, and $n(S)$ denotes number of elements in sample space S.

12 Results from Axiomatic approach of probability

From the axiomatic approach we can also obtain the following results of probabilities (All of these correspond to the formulae used in sets):

(i) $P(A') = 1 - P(A)$ or $P(A') + P(A) = 1$

(ii) $P(A \cup B) = P(A) + P(B) - P(A \cap B)$

(iii) $P(A-B) = P(A) - P(A \cap B)$ *or* $P(A \cap B') = P(A) - P(A \cap B)$

(iv) De Morgan's Law:

$$P(A' \cap B') = P(A \cup B)' \quad \textbf{\textit{and}} \quad P(A' \cup B') = P(A \cap B)'$$

(v) $P(A \cup B \cup C) = P(A) + P(B) + P(C) - P(A \cap B) - P(A \cap C) -$

$$P(B \cap C) + P(A \cap B \cap C)$$

In the above formulae, events represented by sets are as follows:

$P(A')$ represents P(not A),

$P(A \cup B)$ represents P(A or B),

$P(A \cap B)$ represents P(A and B),

$P(A' \cap B')$ represents P(neither A nor B),

$P(A' \cup B')$ represents P(not A or not B),

$P(A-B)$ or $P(A \cap B')$ represents P(only A) if there are only two events A and B.

Chapter-18   Supplement

1   POLYNOMIALS

1) $(x+a)(x+b) = x^2 + (a+b)x + ab$

2) $(a+b)^2 = a^2 + b^2 + 2ab$

3) $(a-b)^2 = a^2 + b^2 - 2ab$

4) $(a+b)(a-b) = a^2 - b^2$

5) $(a+b)^3 = a^3 + b^3 + 3ab(a+b)$

$\quad\quad\quad = a^3 + b^3 + 3a^2 b + 3ab^2$

6) $(a-b)^3 = a^3 - b^3 - 3ab(a-b)$

$\quad\quad\quad = a^3 - b^3 - 3a^2 b + 3ab^2$

7) $(a+b+c)^2 = a^2 + b^2 + c^2 + 2ab + 2bc + 2ca$

8) $a^3 + b^3 = (a+b)(a^2 + b^2 - ab)$

9) $a^3 - b^3 = (a-b)(a^2 + b^2 + ab)$

10) $a^3 + b^3 + c^3 - 3abc = (a+b+c)(a^2 + b^2 + c^2 - ab - bc - ca)$

11) If $a+b+c = 0,$ then $a^3 + b^3 + c^3 = 3abc$

2   MENSURATION

2.1   RECTANGLE :
length $= l$ breadth $= b$

(i) **Perimeter** $= 2(l+b)$ (ii) **Area** $= l\,b$

2.2   SQUARE :
Side $= a$

(i) **Perimeter** $= 4a$ (ii) **Area** $= a^2$

2.3   PARALLELOGRAM :
2 adjacent sides are a & b.

(i) **Perimeter** $= 2(a+b)$ (ii) **Area** $= base \times altitude$

---

*Asterisk (*) marked article (if any) is **not** in CBSE 2025-26 syllabus.*

2.4 RHOMBUS :

Side $= a$ and   2 diagonals are d_1 & d_2

(i) Perimeter $= 4a$

(ii) Area = base x altitude   OR   **(iii) Area** $= \dfrac{1}{2} d_1 d_2$

2.5 TRAPEZIUM :

2 parallel sides are: a & b.
Distance between parallel sides $= h$

Area $= \dfrac{1}{2}(a + b) \times h$

2.6 TRIANGLE :

3 sides are a, b & c.

(i) Perimeter $= a + b + c$

(ii) Semi–perimeter, $s = \dfrac{a+b+c}{2}$

(iii) Heron's formula: Area $= \sqrt{s(s-a)(s-b)(s-c)}$

(iv) Area $= \dfrac{1}{2} \times$ base x altitude

2.7 EQUILATERAL TRIANGLE :

Side $= a$

(i) Perimeter $= 3a$ **(ii) Area** $= \dfrac{\sqrt{3}}{4} a^2$

2.8 CIRCLE :

Radius $= r$

(i) Circumference $= 2\pi r$ **(ii) Area** $= \pi r^2$

2.9 SECTOR of a CIRCLE :

Radius $= r$ angle of sector $= \theta$ length of arc $= l$

(i) Length of Arc $= \dfrac{\theta}{360°} \times 2\pi r$

(ii) Area of Sector $= \dfrac{\theta}{360°} \times \pi r^2$

(iii) Area of Sector $= \dfrac{1}{2} \times l \times r$

(iv) Perimeter of Sector $= l + 2r$

2.10 SEGMENT of a CIRCLE :

Radius = r angle subtended at center = θ

(i) Area of minor segment

= Area of minor sector – Area of Δ formed by 2 radii and the chord

(ii) Area of major segment = Area of circle – Area of minor segment

2.11 CUBOID:

Length = l breadth = b height = h

(i) Lateral Surface Area (or Area of 4 walls) = $2h\,(l+b)$

(ii) Total Surface Area = $2(lb+bh+lh)$

(iii) Volume = lbh

(iv) Longest Diagonal = $\sqrt{l^2+b^2+h^2}$

2.12 CUBE:

Edge = a

(i) Lateral Surface Area (or Area of 4 walls) = $4a^2$

(ii) Total Surface Area = $6a^2$

(iii) Volume = a^3

(iv) Longest Diagonal = $a\sqrt{3}$

2.13 CYLINDER:

Radius = r height = h

(i) Curved Surface Area = $2\pi r h$

(ii) Total Surface Area = $2\pi r h + 2\pi r^2$

       OR   **Total Surface Area** = $2\pi r\,(r+h)$

(iii) Volume = $\pi r^2 h$

2.14 CONE:

Radius = r height = h slant height = l

(i) Slant height: $l = \sqrt{h^2+r^2}$

(ii) Curved Surface Area = $\pi r l$

(iii) Total Surface Area = $\pi r l + \pi r^2$

       OR   **Total Surface Area** = $\pi r\,(r+l)$

(iv) Volume = $\dfrac{1}{3}\pi r^2 h$

---

*Asterisk (*) marked article (if any) is **not** in CBSE 2025-26 syllabus.*

2.15 SPHERE:

Radius = r

(i) Total Surface Area $= 4\pi r^2$

(ii) Volume $= \dfrac{4}{3}\pi r^3$

2.16 Hemi SPHERE:

Radius = r

(i) Curved Surface Area $= 2\pi r^2$

(ii) Total Surface Area $= 3\pi r^2$

(iii) Volume $= \dfrac{2}{3}\pi r^3$

2.17 FRUSTUM:

Radii of 2 circular ends are r_1 & r_2.   height $= h$

slant height $= l$

(i) Slant height: $\quad l = \sqrt{h^2 + (r_1 - r_2)^2}$

(ii) Curved Surface Area $= \pi(r_1 + r_2)\,l$

(iii) Total Surface Area $= \pi(r_1 + r_2)\,l + \pi r_1^2 + \pi r_2^2$

(iv) Volume $= \dfrac{1}{3}\pi h(r_1^2 + r_2^2 + r_1 r_2)$

~~~~~~~~~~END~~~~~~~~~~

*Asterisk (*) marked article (if any) is **not** in CBSE 2025-26 syllabus.*
~~~~~~~~~~

www.ingramcontent.com/pod-product-compliance
Lightning Source LLC
Chambersburg PA
CBHW040808150726
48196CB00058B/1457